Myths and Mysteries of the First World War

Leonard James

www.BretwaldaBooks.com
@Bretwaldabooks
bretwaldabooks.blogspot.co.uk/
Bretwalda Books on Facebook

First Published 2014

Bretwalda Books
Unit 8, Fir Tree Close, Epsom,
Surrey KT17 3LD
info@BretwaldaBooks.com
www.BretwaldaBooks.com
ISBN 978-1-909698-41-3

Printed and bound in Great Britain by
Marston Book Services Limited, Oxfordshire

Contents

Introduction

WHEN I WAS A BOY my father used to tell me stories about our family. He himself had served in RAF Bomber Command during the Second World War, but he came from an old military family which has been supplying soldiers to Britain for generations. Among those soldiers were several who campaigned in the First World War.

Great Uncle George was the hero of the family. He had gone out to France within days of war being delared. He marched up to Mons in that lovely August of 1914 to fight the Germans, then he had slogged back through the terrible Retreat from Mons before turning to fight on the Marne. It was there that he was promoted to sergeant on the field of battle for his leadership - his company having no officers left after the heavy casualties taken on the long retreat.

George fought in many of the major battles that followed. He won a fistful of medals to prove his devotion to duty and his bravery. He ended the war training American "Doughboys" as they came off the ship from the States, teaching them the murderous reality of trench warfare that was so very different from the type of warfare envisaged at West Point. There were other men of the family on the Western Front. Charles who died after his leg was blown off by a German shell, and Edward who came through without a scratch.

As a boy I lapped up the tales. How George was nearly caught by Uhlans on the Retreat from Mons. How a patrol went wrong. About the bread in the trenches. But my father also passed on to me other stories. The Angel of Mons was one of the first, that and the career of the Red Baron. Of how the rank and file drank cheap local wine in cafes and came to call the local *vin blanc* "plonk" - so coining a phrase for cheap wine that would last for decades.

When I grew older I, like many others, had other concerns to deal with. But those childhood tales of our family's involvement in the great wars of the 20th century never really left me.

With the approach of the Centenary of the First World War, I was reminded of those tales from my childhood. Television shows and books began to appear, but interesting and informative as they all are there seemed to be a gap. Where was the Angel of Mons? Where was the Red Baron?

I thought it might be time to have a look at the myths and mysteries of the Great War our ancestors fought a century ago. There turned out to be more than I had thought, and this book is the result. You will find not just an angel, but ghosts, disappearances, spies, wanderers and phantoms. Some of the myths have been debunked, some of the mysteries have been solved. Others have not. Some of the mysteries that puzzled people then remain puzzles today.

Of course battle is a terrible thing. It imposes severe strains on the men who fight. They are frequently physically exhausted and often under enormous psychological pressure. Men in battle are susceptible to fancies and to fallacies. They clutch at straws of hope and plunge into the depths of despair. Perhaps they are more prone to see things that are not there, or at least to believe that other people may have done so. Or maybe it is that men do strange things in battle, creating mysteries every bit as bizarre as they are real.

Anyway, I have done my best to research the old legends and mysteries. I have sought to find solutions when I can or to give the facts as they are known when I can't. Make of this book what you will, but honour the men who fought.

Hope you enjoy it,

Leonard James.

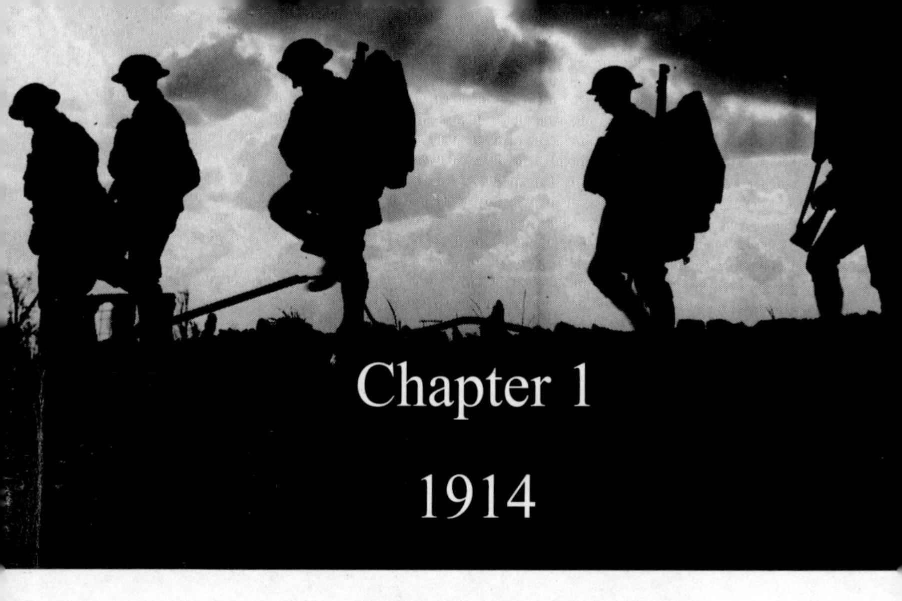

Chapter 1

1914

Who Killed the Archduke?

THE FIRST AND PERHAPS THE GREATEST MYSTERY of the First World War concerns its outbreak. The great states of Europe - Britain, France and Russia on one side against Germany and Austria-Hungary on the other - declared war against each other between 28 July and 4 August 1914.

Officially the reasons for the outbreak of war were the demands that Austria-Hungary put on the Kingdom of Serbia after a Serb murdered Archduke Franz Ferdinand, heir to the Austrian throne in Sarajevo on 28 June. Tensions had been building between the great powers in general, and between Austria-Hungary and Serbia in particular, for some months. The commonly accepted version of events is that the murder in Sarajevo was the spark that inadvertently set off a chain of events that brought all the great powers to the fields of war.

But even at the time not everyone accepted this version of events. When war broke out the mystery of what had actually happened was forgotten in the rush to war and the insistent demands of armies in battle. But the questions being raised in

Archduke Franz Ferdinand and his wife Sophie arriving at the Town Hall of Sarajevo in Bosnia on the day of the assassination.

July 1914 have never really been answered and the mystery remains.

The fact is that Archduke Franz Ferdinand was not a popular man at the Hapsburg court, nor in the corridors of power of the Austrian government. He was arrogant, convinced he was right about everything, intolerant of opinions he did not like and - which made things worse - not particularly clever. The senior bureaucrats in the Austro-Hungarian Empire dreaded the day when he would become Emperor. And that day was not far off.

Emperor Franz Joseph had sat on the throne since 1848. He was old, sick and clearly not long for this world. And he had fallen out badly with his nephew Franz Ferdinand. The event that made the two men fall out came in 1896 when Franz

Ferdinand, then aged just 21, announced that he wanted to marry Countess Sophie Chotek. The Countess was young, pretty and intelligent and came from a family that had been of noble blood in Bohemia for at least the past 600 years. But that was not good enough for the elderly Franz Joseph. He declared that his nephew had to marry a royal princess to begat an Imperial heir of unalloyed blue blood. What the young man did for leisure was of little concern, he could have all the girlfriends he wanted, but he had to marry a princess.

Young Franz Ferdinand refused. He wanted to marry Sophie and that was that. In the end the Emperor allowed the marriage to go ahead, but on the humiliating terms that Franz Ferdinand's wife would be denied the title of Archduchess, retaining her own rank, and that her children were barred from inheriting the throne. Whenever a court event demanded that Franz Ferdinand attend, he was put on the top table, his wife consigned to a side aisle.

It was humiliating and the younger couple grew bitter. They detested the bureaucrats and nobles close to the old emperor. Franz Ferdinand made no secret of the fact he would sack the lot as soon as he came to power.

Politically Franz Ferdinad was a direct threat to the policies being followed by the government in Vienna. Traditionally the Hapsburgs had ruled their vast domains through a diffused system. The Emperor of Austria was also Duke of Dalmatia, but Dalmatia had its own government - as did more than a dozen other states ruled by the elder Emperor. For some 30 years there had been a slow but determined drive to unify the Empire into a single, monolithic state. Franz Joseph supported the changes, Franz Ferdinand did not.

Both men recognised that the changes alienated some of the Empire's citizens and alarmed smaller countries on the Empire's borders - of which the Kingdom of Serbia was one. They differed over how to deal with the situation. Franz Ferdinand wanted to go back to the dispersed system of government. Franz Joseph put in place strict security systems to crack down on dissent and bully smaller states into silence.

In 1908 the small state of Bosnia had its nominal independence stripped away and it was thenceforth ruled direct from Vienna. Thc largely Serb population of Bosnia resented the move. The Kingdom of Serbia feared it would be next.

Various groups were formed to campaign for Serb freedoms, Serb culture and Serb power. Most were peaceful, but one was dedicated to violence. The Black Hand was made up of serving or former members of the Serb Army. They undertook terrorist attacks on Austrian government posts in Bosnia.

In May 1914 it was announced that Franz Ferdinand would visit Sarajevo, capital of Bosnia, on 28 June to undertake assorted ceremonial duties. The Black Hand decided to kill him. Not long afterwards rumours began to circulate in Vienna that the heir to the throne would not be coming back from Sarajevo - there would be an accident of some kind. That would clear the way for Archdule Karl, a grandnephew of the elderly Emperor, to become heir to the throne. Karl was a jovial figure who shared the views and policies of the Austrian government. And he had married an Italian princess.

It has never been explained why Archduke Franz Ferdinand's trip to Sarajevo went ahead when it did. There was nothing urgent that he had to attend to, merely some routine ceremonial duties. When he got there Franz Ferdinand found that the military escort that he had expected was not there. Even worse, the three special police officers assigned as bodyguards were separated from him by a local police officer and left in a waiting room at the railway station.

Meanwhile Franz Ferdinand and Sophie were driving in an open-topped car through the city streets. As they passed a bridge a member of the Black Hand named Nedeljko Čabrinović threw a handgrenade. It bounced off the car and exploded in the road. About 20 people were injured, but the Archduke and his wife were uninjured.

As his visit ended, Franz Ferdinand could still not find his bodyguards. He decided to avoid the planned route - fearing more assassins - and instead told the driver to stick to the main roads and head straight to the station. The driver did no such thing. Claiming that he "got lost" the driver went straight back to the scene of the earlier attack. There another Black Hand man, Gavrilo Princip, was waiting. He lunged forward and shot both Franz Ferdinand and Sophie.

Despite swift medical attention, both victims died within the hour.

Both Čabrinović and Princip were arrested by the Austrian police, put on trial, convicted of murder and sentenced to 20 years in prison. Čabrinović promptly vanished. The Austrian authorities later claimed that he had died in prison of tuberculosis and been hurriedly buried in a secret grave.

By that time a rumour was circulating in Serbia that Čabrinović had been an Austrian agent all along. Several members of the Black Hand had, apparently, harboured suspicions about him from the moment he had volunteered in 1912. It was alleged that he had not died in prison, but had been released with a new identity and the pay for his work.

Meanwhile, the Austrian government had got exactly what it wanted. Franz Ferdinand was no longer going to be Emperor, the much more amenable Karl was heading for the throne instead. Just as important Austria-Hungary had a perfect excuse to engineer a war against Serbia. Which is exactly what they did.

On the Kaiser's Yacht

WHEN THE WAR WAS OVER and the victor's were writing the history books, they unanimously blamed Germany's Kaiser Wilhelm II for the outbreak of the war. The Kaiser was indignant, saying that he had done everything he could do to try avoid a war.

So what exactly was the Kaiser's role in the July Crisis and why has it remained a mystery to this day?

Kaiser Wilhelm was a complex man. He was clever to the point of brilliance, romantic, sentimental, kind to friends, but at the same time arrogant, rash and impatient. Above all he wanted to do what was right for Germany. He saw Germany's future as an industrial powerhouse, so he took a close interest in new inventions, but also as a world power, so he took an equally close interest in his army and navy. What he saw as a necessary expansion of German military might to protect its commercial interests, others saw as a threat to peace.

In foreign affairs, Wilhelm had frequently acted in a confrontational way. Smaller states saw him as a bully to be feared, large countries as a bully to be faced down. But he was no fool. In 1911 he sent a German warship to the Moroccan port of Agadir to "protect German interests" at a time when the pro-French Sultan was under siege in his palace from an Islamic mob. Wilhelm both wanted to discomfit France and demonstrate to the Turkish Ottoman Empire that he was a friend to Islam. But when a British battleship arrived off the coast, supported by cruisers and destroyers, Wilhelm backed down. Posturing had not worked, but there was always next time and in the meanwhile he did not want a war.

When the news of the assassination of Archduke Franz Ferdinand reached Germany, Kaiser Wilhelm sent messages of sympathy to the newly orphaned children, to the Hapsburg family and to Austria-Hungary. He also sent a private telegram to Count Heinrich von Tschirschky, German ambassador in Vienna, telling him to deliver a message to Austrian Foreign Minister Count Leopold Berchtold. The message was simple "You should take no hasty measures in settling accounts with Serbia".

Berchtold responded by sending his chief civil servant Alexander Hoyos to Berlin to see the Kaiser. Hoyos took with him a letter drafted by Berchtold and signed by Emperor Franz Joseph. The letter covered several pages, recounting how the different countries of the Balkans and eastern Europe had reacted to the assassination and giving an appraisal of whether those countries were friendly or hostile to Austria-Hungary and its ally Germany. Russia and Serbia were painted in very hostile terms, the rest as friends (such as Greece) or neutrals (for instance Romania).

Crucially the letter ended by painting a rosy view of future friendship and support throughout East Europe, then continued " But this will not be possible unless Serbia which is at present the pivot of Pan-Slavist policy is eliminated as a political factor in the Balkans. In these conditions Austria-Hungary must tear away with a strong hand the net in which its enemy seeks to entangle it."

Hoyos arrived in Berlin on 5 July and went to the Hapsburg Embassy where he met ambassador Count L. de Szogyeny-Marich. The two men then went to see the Kaiser at his Potsdam Palace. The meeting lasted a long time. When it was over, Hoyos got straight back on a train to Vienna. When he arrived he jubilantly declared that the Kaiser had given Austria-Hungary "a blank cheque" to do whatever it liked with Serbia and that Germany would support them to the hilt.

Next day, however, Berchtold received a telegram from the German Chancellor Theobald von Bethmann-Hollweg which

Kaiser Wilhelm II (centre) with Generals Hindenburg (left) and Ludendorff studying a map. The Prussian military tradition and Wilhelm's truculent diplomacy have often been blamed for the war, but was that fair?

had been sent a few hours after Hoyos left Berlin. Bethmann-Hollweg and the Kaiser had held a discussion about the Serbian situation and the telegram was the result. It briefly recapitulated the situation in the Balkans then it concluded "Finally, as far as concerns Serbia, His Majesty, of course, cannot interfere in the dispute now going on between Austria-Hungary and that country, as it is a matter not within his competence. The Emperor Francis Joseph may, however, rest assured that His Majesty will faithfully stand by Austria-Hungary, as is required by the obligations of his alliance and of his ancient friendship."

The alliance to which Bethmann-Hollweg referred was that agreed between Germany and the Hapsburgs in 1882 by which they agreed to declare war on any country which launched an unprovoked attack on the other. But Austria-Hungary was considering an attack on Serbia, and was not the victim of an attack herself. It was hardly the "blank cheque" that Berchtold had triumphantly announced.

Having seen Bethmann-Hollweg send the telegram, Kaiser Wilhelm went off on holiday. He usually spent several weeks each summer crusing the Baltic and North Seas in his yacht, stopping off at ports to see the sights, catch up with old friends and relax. He saw no reason not to go on holiday in 1914.

On 24 July the radio operator on board the Kaiser's yacht decided to go ashore for a stroll around Oslo. He stopped at a newstand to ask if they had a German newspaper, but as soon as he saw the headlines he turned and bolted back to the yacht demanding to see the Kaiser. The newspaper carried the text of an ultimatum sent by Austria-Hungary to Serbia. The ultimatum was couched in such terms that Serbia could not agree and remain an independent kingdom.

The Kaiser at once realised the importance of the ultimatum and orderd his yacht to return to the nearest German port. There he commandeered a train and headed for Berlin at full speed. He was met on the station platform by an ashen-faced Bethmann-Hollweg.

"How did this all happen?" demanded the Kaiser.

"This duplicity of Austria is intolerable," came the reply.

The two men did not know it, but the Serbian army had already been mobilised and Austrian troops were marching toward the Serb border.

Later that day the reply of the Serb King Peter arrived in Berlin. Kaiser Wilhelm relaxed. King Peter had agreed to most of the Austrian demands, and those that he had not accepted outright he had suggested the two sides refer to the International Court at the Hague.

The Kaiser sent a telegram to Emperor Franz Joseph: "Serbia has in fact met the Austrian demands in so wide-sweeping a manner that if the Austro-Hungarian Government adopted a wholly uncompromising attitude, a gradual revulsion of public opinion against it in all of Europe would have to be reckoned with."

But Tsar Nicholas II was convinced that the Austro-Hungarians were going to invade Serbia anyway. As an ally of Serbia he ordered the Russian army to mobilise on 26 July and take up positions on his borders with the Hapsburg Empire.

King Peter of Serbia rides in state through the streets of his capital, Belgrade. Peter and his government felt that they had sidestepped Austro-Hungarian belligerance with their reply to the ultimatu. They were wrong.

Nicholas contacted his ally the French Republic to ask for support if Germany were to attack. France began mobilising its army on 27 July.

At 11am on 28 July King Peter of Serbia received a telegram which read "The Royal Serbian Government not having answered in a satisfactory manner the note of July 23, 1914, presented by the Austro-Hungarian Minister at Belgrade, the Imperial and Royal Government are themselves compelled to see to the safeguarding of their rights and interests, and, with this object, to have recourse to force of arms. Austria-Hungary consequently considers herself henceforward in a state of war with Serbia."

He thought it was a hoax and insisted that the source of the message be traced back by the telegraph engineers. The investigation was still incomplete when the Austrian artillery opened fire.

On 29 July the Kaiser learned that Russian troops were being mobilised close to the German border. He telegraphed Tsar Nicholas asking him to pull the troops back and promised to contact Emperor Franz Joseph to try to talk sense into him. Tsar Nicholas agreed, and moved his troops toward Austria instead. The Kaiser's telegrams sent that day to Austria went ominously unanswered.

On 30 July the Kaiser tried again. He and Bethmann-Hollweg sent a string of increasingly frantic telegrams to Vienna. They urged Austria-Hungary to stop once they had captured the key border forts. They urged Austria-Hungary to accept mediation from a neutral country. They urged Austria-Hungary to agree a cease fire for humanitarian reasons to allow civilians to flee the war zone.

At 5pm Franz Joseph finally responded. He ordered full mobilisation of his army, navy and reserves, sending troops to march to the Russian border. Tsar Nicholas responded by fully mobilising his forces, and resuming the build up of troops along the German border.

Kaiser Wilhelm heard of the Russian action next morning on 31 July. He ordered full German mobilisation and sent off two telegrams. The first was to Tsar Nicholas asking him to move his troops away from the German border, the second was to France asking them to remain neutral in any war between Germany and Russia. The French responded by announcing a full mobilisation.

Kaiser Wilhelm was in a serious quandry. The German army currently under arms was larger, better trained and better equipped than any other in Europe, but France and Russia had vastly larger reserves. If he waited until his enemies were fully mobilised - a process that would take weeks - the German army would be swamped by numbers. If he struck at once he stood a chance of gaining a swift victory. Concluding Germany's only chance of victory in a pan-European war was to march quickly, Wilhelm declared war on Russia on 1 August and on France two days later.

In 1870 German armies had invaded France and crushed the French armies in a matter of days. Since then the French had built powerful forts along the border that would slow down, and probably stop, any German attack. A swift victory could be gained only if the German armies marched around the flank of the forts, which meant going through Belgium.

Kaiser Wilhelm asked King Albert I of Belgium for permission to march through his lands. Albert refused. The Germans invaded anyway on 4 August. Belgian neutrality had been guaranteed by Germany, France and Britain by treaty. The British ambassador in Berlin, Sir Edward Goschen went to see Bethmann-Hollweg later that day and demanded the German troops withdraw from Belgium. The German chancellor was almost in tears. He paced constantly up and down the room, fidgeting with pieces of paper and rubbing his head with his hands. He kept up a monologue asking Goschen why the Russians were so intent on war, why the French had not declared neutrality, why the Austrian's were such fools. Clearly he was not really listening to Goschen. Nevertheless Goschen made it clear that if Germany did not pull out of Belgium, Britain would declare war. Bethmann-Hollweg stared at him. "Great Britain would go to make war on a kindred nation who desired nothing better than to be friends with her?" he asked in disbelief. He slumped over his desk and lapsed into silence. Goschen left. Britain joined the war next day.

It is certain that my his posturing, bullying and arrogant behaviour Kaiser Wilhelm had done much to raise the tensions in Europe during the years leading up to 1914. But whether or not he had been a factor in the actual outbreak of war depends very much on what happened during his meeting at Potsdam Palace with Hoyos and Szogyeny-Marich on 4 July. If he had given the Austrians a blank cheque then he had effectively told them to invade Serbia. If not then he was innocent of having started the war.

It is impossible to know for certain what happened at Potsdam. Neither the Germans nor Austrians took written notes - which is very unusual for such top level discussions in a crisis and is in itself suspicious. Hoyos was always adamant that Austria-Hungary had been given the notorious "blank cheque" to do what it liked with Serbia and would have German support. Kaiser Wilhelm forever insisted that he had done no such thing.

All that can be said is that Hoyos behaved as if he had been given a blank cheque, while Wilhelm behaved as if he had not. Perhaps there had been a misunderstanding, though that seems rather unlikely. On balance it would seem that Hoyos heard what he wanted to hear, or perhaps he deliberately misrepresented what was said.

Given the actions of the Austro-Hungarian government it seems, on balance, more likely that they deliberately set up the Germans and tricked them into supporting action against Serbia that Wilhelm in fact opposed.

But solving the mystery of who was to blame for the outbreak of war only gives rise to another: What on Earth were the Austrians up to? When it had all gone horribly wrong, of course, nobody was going to admit that they had been to blame, or even what had really been done.

The answer can probably be found in comments made by senior Austro-Hungarian officials before the outbreak of war. The clearest of these came from Wilhelm Ritter von Storck, Hapsburg ambassador to Serbia a few days after the assassination of Franz Ferdinand. He cabled Vienna "Serbia must learn to fear us again. Otherwise, our old border regions, and not just the annexed provinces, will be in danger."

Undoubtedly this reflected the thinking among senior bureaucrats in Vienna. The various peoples in the Hapsburg Empire were becoming increasingly aware of their own nationality and less tolerant of rule by a foreign dynasty. The preferred response of the Empire was to smack them down, and to do so hard. The Austro-Hungarian government wanted to crush Serbia not only to removed the Serb threat but also to teach others a lesson. But they were fully aware that Russia would not tolerate an independent Slav kingdom being destroyed in this way. An invasion of Serbia would inevitably lead to war with Russia.

Russia was a powerful empire. While Austria-Hungary might have been able to defeat Russia, such an outcome was by no means certain and would in any case involve the Hapsburgs in great losses of men and money. It seems almost certain that the Austrian bureaucrats calculated that if they had German support Tsar Nicholas would not attack. They were using the threat of

German intervention to stop a war with Russia breaking out. Instead they precipitated a world wide conflict of epic proportions.

Which in turn leads to another mystery. If it were Austria-Hungary that was responsible for the outbreak of the First World War, why was almost the entire world so vociferous in blaming Germany? The answer to that mystery belongs more properly to the chapter on 1918.

What was important in 1914 was that the world was at war.

Who Killed the Ambassador?

While Europe watched the events in the Balkans and waited to see what would happen, another mystery unfolded. It was largely ignored by the wider world, but would have a profound effect on the events that led to war.

On 10 July Nicholas Hartwig, Russian Ambassador to Serbia, was invited to lunch with Baron von Giesl, Austro-Hungarian Ambassador to Serbia. The two men enjoyed a good lunch during which they discussed the assassination of Archduke Franz Ferdinand and the possible repercussions. They parted on good terms, but less than an hour later Hartwig was dead. He was aged only 57 and in robust good health.

Within hours the Serb press were were quoting an unnamed source at the Russian Embassy accusing the Austrians of having poisoned Hartwig during the lunch. It must be admitted that the Austrians had very good reason to want to get rid of Hartwig.

Hartwig had been Ambassador to Serbia since 1909. His background was among the minor nobility, but his intelligence and talents had secured him rapid promotion and by 1909 he was one of the most senior diplomats in Russia. His appointment to Serbia was an indication of how important Tsar Nicholas considered his relations with King Peter to be.

It was soon proved that Serb-Russian relations were not only important, but volatile. The Islamic Ottoman Empire was in decline, riven by corruption and economic decline. The small Christian states of the Balkans, by contrast, were in the ascendancy with booming economies and well run governments. The Balkan provinces of the Ottomans were populated mostly by Greeks, Serbs and Bulgarians who agitated not only for religious freedoms, but also for nationalist freedoms. In 1912 the Christian kingdoms attacked the Ottomans, winning a swift victory and seizing almost all the Balkans. The victors then fell out with each other over the division of the captured lands and fought a short war in 1913 to sort things out.

Throughout these tense years, Hartwig struggled to ensure the wider cause of Russian friendship with the Christian states remained constant. He cultivated contacts in all the Balkan states, encouraging links to Russia and fostering cultural sympathies through dances, concerts and dinners. He was a famously wily diplomat and charming man. If anyone would be astute enough to see a way through the trap Austria-Hungary was laying for Serbia, and charming enough to get people to agree to it, that man was Hartwig. From the Austrian point of view, Hartwig had to go.

And go he did with suspicious suddenness.

By the time suspicions began to be raised about his death, events were moving on fast. Everyone was too busy to wonder about his sudden demise. He was buried and forgotten.

There is no real evidence that the powerful cabal within the Austro-Hungarian government that was determined on war with Serbia had murdered Hartwig, any more than that they had murdered Franz Ferdinand. However the two deaths were both very sudden and both very convenient - and both men had died in close proximity to Austrian officials.

When the Lamps Went Out

One of the most famous quotes from 1914 was said by the British Foreign Secretary Sir Edward Grey on 3 August 1914. Unfortunately it is not entirely clear that he ever uttered the words ascribed to him.

The Foreign Office from Horse Guards Road as it was in 1914. Sir Edward Grey is supposed to have been looking out of a first floor window on this facade when he spoke his famous words.

By 3 August Austria-Hungary was at war with Serbia and Russia, Germany at war with Russia and France, and German troops were marching towards Belgium, an act that would bring Britain into the war. The conflict that was then starting was quite clearly going to be fought on an epic scale, would cost untold numbers of human lives and vast sums of money. The economies of Europe would be destroyed, Empires laid waste and civilisation itself put under severe strain.

That evening Sir Edward Grey was working late in his office at the Foreign Office in Westminster. At about 8pm he welcomed to his office for a short meeting John Alfred Spender, the editor of the newspaper Westminster Gazette which was influential and widely read among the nobility and establishment. Grey outlined the latest events and the attitude of the British government.

As he talked Grey moved to the window, looking out across St James's Park toward The Mall and Buckingham Palace where King George V waited anxiously to know if his country would be going to war.

As he gazed out across the twilit scene the newly installed electric lights along The Mall began to glow as they flickered into life. Spender came to stand beside him. Grey pointed at the scene and remarked "The lamps are going out all over Europe, we shall not see them lit again in our life-time." It was a poignant and moving moment.

The problem is that Grey could not remember the incident. In 1925 he was pressed about the remark which by then had become very famous. He carefully avoided giving a direct response, instead saying:

"A friend came to see me on one of the evenings of the last week — he thinks it was on Monday, August 3rd. We were standing at a window of my room in the Foreign Office. It was getting dusk, and the lamps were being lit in the space below on which we were looking. My friend recalls that I remarked on this with the words: 'The lamps are going out all over Europe, we shall not see them lit again in our life-time.'"

Grey was not known for his modesty, so it is strange that he did not lay claim to the quote by which he was most widely known - unless of course he never said it. Spender was an editor with a newspaper to sell. Nobody ever accused him of actually fabricating a story, but embellishing one was not beyond him.

Sir Edward Grey goes fishing

One of the more enduring stories about Britain's entry into the First World War is that Foreign Secretary, Sir Edward Grey, took the decision while out fishing in Hampshire.

Sir Edward Grey heard on Saturday 1 August that Germany had declared war on Russia. Most diplomats realised that this would mean that war would break out between France and Germany within days. The question that faced Grey was what Britain should do.

Britain had a series of treaties and agreements with Russia and with France relating to trade, colonies and cultural links. None of those agreements involved any form of a military alliance, nor a commitment to support France or Russia in a war.

Relations with Germany were more difficult. Kaiser Wilhelm had made it clear that he wanted Germany to use its large and growing economic and military might to propel the country into being a major world power. That Germany had territorial ambitions in Europe was a concern, but the real worry for Britain lay overseas. Germany had been since 1897 building a large and modern war fleet. Kaiser Wilhelm wanted to have a fleet two thirds the size of Britain's. Officially this was to safeguard German merchant ships at sea and secure communications with overseas colonies. In fact it was to ensure that Britain could not use its control of the oceans to strangle German trade in the event of a war. Germany had backed down in the face of British naval threats before and Wilhelm wanted to be in a position to make Britain think twice before making such a threat again.

In Britain the massive build up of German naval power was seen as a direct threat, while Germany's growing influence in the Middle East and eastern Europe was a more distant, but still serious concern.

Nobody in the British government could decide if Britain should join the unfolding European war. To join would involve much loss of life and cost a huge sum of money. To stay out would mean Britain's trade would be seriously disrupted and much money and lives would be expended protecting Britain's neutrality and her shipping. Moreover, Britain's warm relationships with friendly France and Russia would be put at risk if Britain stuck to the letter, but not the spirit of her agreements. Whatever Britain did, the consequences would be immense.

According to the story, Sir Edward Grey left a cabinet meeting held on 1 August and instead of going home boarded a train for Hampshire. He made his way to a small fishing cottage that he rented beside the River Itchen at Itchen Abbas. The next day, Sunday 2 August, Grey picked up his fishing rods and strolled down to the banks of the Itchen. He spent the day fly fishing, mulling things over in his mind. As dusk fell, Grey made up his mind. He packed away his rods and caught the train back to London.

Next day he told the Cabinet that he believed that Britain should join the war on the side of France and Russia. Having got their agreement he went to the House of Commons and delivered perhaps the finest speech of his life. The vote was for war.

Whether there is any truth in the story is hard to tell. Grey was a devoted fisherman - he even wrote books on the subject - and he did go down to his cottage in Hampshire whenever he could. However, given the fast moving nature of the unfolding crisis it seems unlikely that the Foreign Secretary would want to be out of touch with either his fellow ministers or with news from abroad for an entire day to go fishing. Nor is there any evidence that he was away from London for so long.

Perhaps it is just a legend after all.

Belgian Atrocities

On 4 August 1914 vast German armies marched over the Belgian border on their way to invade France. Within days both sides would be screaming about "atrocities" committed in Belgium.

A key objective was the city of Liege, a central hub of the Belgian railway system. The Germans needed the Belgian railways to transport supplies to their armies, so Liege had to be captured. The Belgians knew the value of the city's railways, so they had surrounded them with forts built of steel and concrete, equipped with artillery and machine guns. The forts held out until 16 August, delaying the German advance for a few crucial days. The delay infuriated the Germans.

The resistance of Liege meant that the Belgian government in Brussels had time to mobilise its army for war, even though large tracts of land were already over run by the Germans. Many reservists hurried to their mobilisation depots only to find them already under German control. They then set off to walk to

The monument erected in Dinant after the war to the 674 civilians killed in the town by the Germans as they marched through in August 1914.

somewhere free of German troops where they could muster to the colours. A good number of these men carried their rifles as they walked, but did not have a uniform. Inevitably some of these men got into fire fights with Germans. Other Belgian soldiers in civilian clothing were caught cutting telegraph wires.

The reaction of the Germans was swift and fierce. It was against the rules of war for men not in uniform to take part in battle. The Germans loudly accused the Belgian government of deliberately organising flying columns of civilian clad soldiers to ambush German troops. It was, the Germans said, an "atrocity of war" - the first use of such a phrase. Any man caught in civilian clothes and carrying a gun would be shot as a spy.

There were other incidents about which the Germans complained. A German general had got out of his motor car to visit a unit when a young Belgian woman walked up to the parked car. She smiled at the driver, then pulled out a pistol and blew his brains out. The Germans said they were minded to be merciful to the woman on account of her age and the fact that her fiancee had been killed in the early fighting.

Less easy to forgive were the more definite atrocities. A German soldier was found lying in a ditch with his hands tied and a bullet hole in his head. Clearly he had been captured, then killed when helpless.

Such stories flooded the German newspapers, and were picked up in neutral countries. Their impact outside Germany was lessened by the fact that the German military, keen to preserve operational secrecy, refused to confirm the stories or even to say when or where they had taken place.

Undoubtedly the Germans thought that they were acting correctly when they executed out of hand armed men in civilian clothing. By the rules of war as they were then understood, they may well have been justfied, but the sheer scale of the executions and the off hand way they were carried out appalled people in neutral nations. At Aarschot 156 men were shot, at Andenne 211 were put in front of firing squads in a single day and at Tamines 383 were executed in 48 hours. When a railway train was derailed near Leuvan, the local German general had the entire 10,000 strong population of the town driven out at the point of the bayonet and then burned the entire town to the ground - including its famous library of rare medieval manuscripts.

Such acts, which the Germans did nothing to deny as they believed they were behaving correctly, set the ground for what became known as the Belgian Atrocities. These were acts allegedly carried out by the Germans in Belgium.

Most of the stories originated from refugees fleeing to France or to Britain. These tales of atrocities were more convincing than those told by the Germans for they included names, places and dates.

David Tordens, a carter from the village of Sempst, told British reporters waiting on the dockside at Dover that the German army had reached Sempst on 14 August. The villagers had locked themselves in their houses and hoped for the best. The Germans camped in the village square, breaking into the shops to steal food. That evening the Germans got wildly drunk. They smashed down the door to the Tordens household and raped Tordens' wife and 14 year old daughter. When Tordens objected he was beaten unconscious with rifle butts and his son shot dead. Over the next 8 hours every woman in the village was raped, and several men killed.

At Saint-Georges-sur-Meuse on 9 August a German uhlan trooper had killed a six year old boy with his lance after the boy stuck out his tongue. At Heron another young boy had his right hand hacked off by a German on 18 August so that when he grew up he could not be a soldier and fire a rifle. At Brabant a group of nuns was forced to strip naked in front of a jeering German officer who said he thought they might be spies. Some stories did not mention places or dates - such as the German soldier seen roasting a baby over a fire, or another marching down the road with a baby on his bayonet.

What nobody knew at the time, because the British government was keeping the fact very secret, was that the Belgians with stories to tell were being put in front of the reporters by a special unit which had the sole task of spreading propaganda. Based in a town house in Buckingham Gate, London, the unit was led by former MP and journalist Charles Masterman.

In September Prime Minister Asquith responded to public

demands for action by setting up a committee led by the famous historian Viscount Bryce to investigate the stories appearing in the press. The aim was to discover if the tales were true or if the refugees had invented them. The move was rather ironic given that it was Asquith who had hired Masterman. Nevertheless the committe began its work. It interviewed over 1,100 people and reported in May 1915.

The conclusions it came to were that both sides had acted abominably. The report supported German claims that Belgian soldiers in civilian clothes had ambushed German soldiers and carried out sabotage. It also declared to be true many of the stories told by Belgian refugees - including some of the most lurid - though others were dismissed as being without evidence. On balance, it said, the Germans had behaved worst. Rape, murder and looting were routine and frequent occurrences wherever the German army had marched.

Masterman made sure that the report was translated into every European language and more than 41,000 copies were sent to the USA for free distribution. The report had a massive impact on opinion in the USA and in other neutral countries.

In 1920 an historian asked to have access to the transcripts of the interviews that the Bryce Committee had undertaken. He was shown to a storage room in the Home Office. What he found were a few files and notes. There was no evidence at all to support most of the findings of the Report, nor many of the horrific tales it contained. The Home Office explained the files had been accidentally lost.

To this day the truth about the Belgian Atrocities. remains a mystery

The Angel of Mons

ONE OF THE MOST ENDURING LEGENDS from the early weeks of war was of the Angel of Mons - a heavenly figure sent by God to protect the British soldiers in September 1914 when outnumbered by the vast German hordes pouring through Belgium to attack them.

It is difficult to pin down this story with any precision, even though it is one of the best known of the war. The reason for this is simple, it was passed from mouth to mouth, soldier to soldier in oral form for weeks before it started to get into print. By the time it was written down and brought to a wider audience the story had got garbled and details blurred or forgotten. Censorship was strict at this time, with soldiers' letters home being intercepted and all press reports vetted before publication. It was not until soldiers were home on leave that they could tell of their experiences and the stories they had heard.

The rumours of something odd having happened were circulating in the army certainly by November of 1914, and probably in October. It was not until April 1915 that the story appeared in print in Britain. That first version appeared in a magazine devoted to spiritualism. It quoted an unnamed British soldier home on leave who said that "the spirits" had come to the aid of a British unit and had helped them drive off a German attack. More mainstream newspapers then took up the tale. They carried stories, again from anonymous soldiers on leave, that told of angelic assistance. In some versions there was a lone angel, in other versions there was a veritable host, while a few said the heavenly figure had been St George, not an angel at all.

Clergymen and others picked up on the story and began debating whether or not God was taking sides in the war. The horrific stories of Belgian Atrocities were still fresh in many minds, so the idea that God might take a hand against such an evil regime as that of the Kaiser did not seem entirely far fetched.

In June 1915 the stories were investigated by the Society for Psychical Research, an academic body based in London since 1885 which had as its purpose "to examine allegedly paranormal phenomena in a scientific and unbiased way." They found that none of the soldiers put forward by newspapers or others were actual witnesses. They had all heard the story from someone else. One problem was that many of the men who had been interviewed by the press were by this date back in France and so unavailable to be interviewed. The Society declared that the stories of angelic help to British soldiers "prove on investigation to be founded on mere rumour, and cannot be traced to any authoritative source."

In August the author Arthur Machen pointed out that back in September 1914 he had written a short story that had been published by the Evening News newspaper. The story had been titled "The Bowmen" and had told the entirely fictional tale of a British unit assailed by overwhelming German forces. One of the British soldiers prays for salvation and is amazed to see the ghosts of men climbing up out of the ground. These ghosts prove to be the spirits of the archers of the Battle of Agincourt, where England had inflicted a massive defeat on France in 1415. The archers then loose off volleys of arrows at the Germans, who turn and retreat in confusion. Machen claimed his story was the origin of the legend. He then reprinted the story, which sold in huge numbers and made him a nice profit.

Despite this effort at debunking, the story simply would not die. The soldiers in France believed it very firmly and could not be shaken in their belief that something had happened at Mons.

After the war, historian Archie Whitehouse - who had himself

Facing page: The Angel of Mons.

been in France and heard a version of the story - decided to try to get to the bottom of what had happened. He spoke to some of the very few men who had fought at Mons and who had survived the war. They had all heard about the Angel of Mons, but none of them claimed to have actually seen it. A handful, however, did claim to have spoken to someone who had actually been present. These were not, therefore, rumours but second hand accounts. They were not as good as eyewitness versions, but they were consistent and credible. Putting them together, Whitehouse believed he had solved the mystery of what happened.

First he found that the Angel had not appeared at Mons, nor during the fighting around that town. It had appeared during the arduous Retreat from Mons. On 22 August the British Army in Belgium had been attacked by larger German forces at Mons. The British had driven off those attacks, but because French units to the south had given way the British had to retreat. That withdrawal turned into a nightmare march carried out day and night to avoid being outflanked, surrounded and forced to surrender by the German forces pouring through the gap in the French lines.

The retreat lasted for days, with units getting muddled with each other, split apart and confused. Supply wagons were lost, rest was impossible and water was scarce. The men were tired, hungry and confused. Many grumbled that they were retreating even though they had won the fight at Mons. Others were too tired even to talk. Some slept as they marched, their legs continuing to work even as their minds dozed.

On the seventh day of the retreat a group of Coldstream Guards, along with some stragglers from other regiments, found themselves in woodland near Mormal. The only officer present was a young lieutenant, and he had no map and no compass. The group of tired, exhausted and thirsty men were utterly lost.

Gunfire echoed around from the distance, and rifle shots were heard close at hand. The German army was almost upon them.

As darkness fell the men saw the lights of cooking fires only a few hundred feet away. Germans! The lieutenant ordered the men to dig foxholes from which they could fight the advancing German hordes when dawn came. The tired men went to work by starlight, though some simply collapsed in sleep.

A little before midnight one of the men saw a light moving through the trees. He called his sergeant. For a minute or so the two men watched as the yellowish light moved about. Sometimes it vanished behind a tree or bush for a few seconds, but it always reappeared and was getting closer. The sergeant sent the man to fetch the lieutenant. The officer arrived just as the light emerged from the trees. It was the luminous figure of a beautiful, elegant human gleaming with a strange, yellow glow. The officer ordered all the men to be roused and brought to him.

The strange figure came forward toward the men. Then it stopped. By now the men could see that the glowing figure was that of a graceful woman. Some thought she had a gold belt, or gold braid in her hair. A few thought they saw wings, but kept quiet unless their comrades thought them mad.

The figure began to beckon. At first she beckoned slowly, then with more urgency.

The lieutenant went to investigate but had taken only a few steps when he realised that all the men were following him, walking in silence over the grass.

The strange figure then moved off to the left, carefully keeping ahead of the soldiers, but turning every few steps to make sure that they were following. Then she stopped and pointed. The men looked and saw she was pointing along a sunken lane. The figure moved again, going down into the sunken lane and heading southwest.

The men followed the figure along the lane. On either side they could see campfires and hear men moving about. Once they heard a shout in German, but they kept on moving. They had gone about half a mile when the glowing figure abruptly vanished. The men were alone.

Nervously the abandoned men peered about. There were no campfires, no sounds of movement. Hurriedly the lieutenant led them off down the road. Half an hour later they came across a British outpost. They were back with the British army.

Whitehouse believed that this was the original form of the story of the Angel of Mons. The men were, he noted, "weary, battle-tortured men whose minds were fertile soil for any kind of hallucination", though it could not be denied that they had somehow managed to sneak through the entire German army without being seen.

Assuming that Whitehouse was correct and that this version of events was the true one, there seem to be two possible explanations. It might be that an angel of the Lord came to save a squad of British soldiers. On the other hand it may be that a local woman carrying a lantern showed the soldiers a route that she knew would take them past the German camps.

The Officer with a Drum

ANOTHER STORY THAT WAS DOING THE ROUNDS in the British Army in France at the same time as the tale of the Angel of Mons was that of the "Officer with a Drum".

According to the most widely related version of the tale, a British regiment was in severe trouble. They had beaten off German attack after German attack and taken heavy casualties. The men were exhausted, the ammunition almost exhausted and the colonel dead. As the British soldiers gazed with tired eyes at the vast German hordes forming up for a new attack a bizarre figure appeared. Marching up the road toward them came a lone British officer playing a drum. Beating the insistent rhythm of the call "to arms" the officer rallied the ranks and pulled the men to attention. He then ordered the men to pour a succession of volleys of rifle fire at Germans, smashing their formation and tumbling them into retreat.

Then the strange officer picked up his drum again and playing a well known march led the tired men back in retreat and away from the Germans to reach safety.

The tale contains several features in common with the Angel of Mons. First the story is placed during the Retreat from Mons, second it relates how a demoralised British unit was saved from certain destruction and third it is rather vague as to the unit involved. The story may well have been dismissed in much the same way as many people dismissed the story of the Angel, except that the officer concerned survived and wrote his own account of the incident.

On 26 August the commander of the British II Corps, General Horace Smith-Dorrien, ordered his men to stand and fight the advancing German units at Le Cateau. Smith-Dorrien believed that the rapid German advance meant that the Germans had got ahead of their supplies and become disordered. He thought that by mounting a vigorous defence for one day he would force the Germans to hold back and so gain him more time to complete his retreat south toward the distant line of the River Marne.

The plan worked, with the Germans suffering heavy casualties and being forced to halt their advance. However, three British regiments had taken very heavy casualties and become fragmented - the 2nd Suffolks, 1st King's Own and 2nd Royal Irish. Stragglers from all three regiments, and others, were dispersed across the battlefield with many being taken prisoner and others moving south in disordered groups. These men got to the town of St Quentin where they slumped down in exhausted, hungry groups. Capture by the advancing Germans seemed inevitable.

It was at this point that Major Tom Bridges of the 4th Dragoon Guards and his bugler arrived on the scene. They had been sent by Smith-Dorrien to scout the advancing Germans, but instead found the stragglers. Bridges quickly got a few wagons moving south, and then faced the exhausted men slumped in the village square. Bridges recorded what happened next:

> *"The men in the square were a different problem, and so jaded it was pathetic to see them. If one only had a band, I thought. Why not? There was a toy shop handy which provided my trumpeter and myself with a tin whistle and a drum, and we marched round and round the fountain where the men were lying like the dead, playing "The British Grenadiers" and beating the drum like mad.*
>
> *"They sat up and began to laugh and even cheer. I stopped playing and made them a short exhortation and told them I was going to take them back to their regiments. They began to stand up and fall in, and eventually we moved slowly off into the night to the music of our improvised band, now reinforced with a couple of mouth-organs. When well clear of the town I tried to delegate my functions to someone else, but the infantry would not let me go. "Don't leave us, major," they cried, "or by God we'll not get anywhere." So on we went, and it was early morning before I got back to my squadron. Our rearguard was unmolested by the Germans, and it looked as if "more haste, less speed" might well have been the description of this part of the retreat."*

When this account was published in a London newspaper some months later, the poet Henry Newbolt was moved to put it into verse

DREARY lay the long road, dreary lay the town,
Lights out and never a glint o' moon:
Weary lay the stragglers, half a thousand down,
Sad sighed the weary big Dragoon.
"Oh! if I'd a drum here to make them take the road again,
Oh! if I'd a fife to wheedle, Come, boys, come!
You that mean to fight it out, wake and take your load again,
Fall in! Fall in! Follow the fife and drum!

Hey, but here's a toy shop, here's a drum for me,
Penny whistles too to play the tune!
Half a thousand dead men soon shall hear and see
We're a band!" said the weary big Dragoon.
"Rubadub! Rubadub! Wake and take the road again,
Wheedle-deedle-deedle-dee, Come, boys, come!
You that mean to fight it out, wake and take your load again,
Fall in! Fall in! Follow the fife and drum!"

Cheerly goes the dark road, cheerly goes the night,
Cheerly goes the blood to keep the beat:
Half a thousand dead men marching on to fight:
With a little penny drum to lift their feet.
Rubadub! Rubadub! Wake and take the road again,
Wheedle-deedle-deedle-dee, Come, boys, come!
You that mean to fight it out, wake and take your load again,
Fall in! Fall in! Follow the fife and drum!

As long as there's an Englishman to ask a tale of me,
As long as I can tell the tale aright,

We'll not forget the penny whistle's wheedle-deedle-dee
And the big Dragoon a-beating down the night,
Rubadub! Rubadub! Wake and take the road again,
Wheedle-deedle-deedle-dee, Come, boys, come!
You that mean to fight it out, wake and take your load again,
Fall in! Fall in! Follow the fife and drum.

Three years later Bridges, by then a Major General, gained further fame. He was in the trenches when an artillery shell landed nearby and smashed his leg. Bridges was taken to hospital where the doctor told him that his right leg would have to be amputated. "Oh, well," muttered Bridges through his pain, "don't waste it. Feed it to Leo." Leo being the regimental mascot, a tame lion.

The Russians in London

LATE IN AUGUST, WHILE THE BRITISH ARMY IN FRANCE was retreating from Mons, a rumour swept through London.

A night porter dozing at King's Cross station had been woken up when an unscheduled train pulled into Platform 4. Moments later another mysterious train pulled into another platform and before long the entire station was hissing with steam as the engines vented their boilers. The porter gazed in confusion and amazement, then walked over to the nearest locomotive.

"Where are your from?" he called up to the driver.

"Liverpool," came the reply.

The porter gazed at the long lines of passenger carriages that now filled the darkened station.

"What are these trains?" asked the still puzzled porter. The driver just shrugged and turned back to his controls.

Suddenly the doors of the trains slammed open and out poured a large force of men wearing strange uniforms and speaking an incomprehensible language. The officers tumbled from the railway carriages, shouting orders in their foreign tongue to get the men formed up in columns. The soldiers then shouldered their arms and marched out of King's Cross, disappearing through the streets of London, heading south out of sight of the amazed porter.

The marching men were seen next marching down Southampton Row. A carter on his way home from a late shift heard them before he saw them. The rhythmic tread of thousands of boots on the road echoed through the night. The man looked about him in surprise, then the head of the marching column came in sight. Rank upon rank of grim-faced men went swinging by, their eyes fixed firmly ahead, their rifles on their shoulders. Nobody spoke, the columns went by in an eerie

Russian infantry on the march in August 1914. These men are advancing into East Prussia from Russia itself.

silence broken only by the steady tramp, tramp, tramp of thousands of boots.

In Aldwych a night watchman was brewing up a pot of tea when he too heard the steady stamp of marching feet. Rank after rank of big men went marching by, not one of whom so much as glanced at him. The watchman said later that it had taken long minutes for the column to march past, officers in front of each unit and sergeants on the flanks.

Next day the three men told their tales to their friends and colleagues. The strange event of the vast number of silent men marching through London at dead of night spread quickly. By 1 September journalists in Fleet Street had heard the tale. The porter, carter and watchman were found and interviewed. They had little enough to tell, but it was a good story. Given the strict censorship imposed on news from the battlefront in France, the reporters were thankful for the event.

Then things took a turn for the unexpected. A man came forward to say that he had been talking to a man in a pub who had seen the column of men passing over Waterloo Bridge. That would make sense. If the soldiers had come into London from the north at King's Cross it made sense for them to leave heading south from Waterloo Station. It was what the man said next that catapulted the story from being an interesting item on the inside pages to being headline news.

Apparently the man in the pub had accosted one of the officers and offered a cigarette. The officer had smiled and taken the smoke.

"What regiment are you?" asked the man in the pub. The officer had just smiled and shrugged. "Where are you from?" asked the man again. This time the officer grinned, took a drag on the cigarette and replied.

"Russia," he said.

The fact that a large force of Russian soldiers had been

marching through London was electrifying. Everyone knew that the Russian Tsar Nicholas had a vast army. Those in the know knew that army to be poorly trained and poorly equipped, but the sheer size of the Russian army could not be denied. It was easy to believe that the Tsar might well have troops to spare, and could well have sent some of them to join the struggle to stop the German invasion of Belgium and France. After all, the stories of the Belgian Atrocities had reached Russia and may have encouraged the Tsar to lend a hand. And if Russian soldiers had been shipped to England they would have arrived via the port of Liverpool.

Soon other versions of the nocturnal soldiers began to appear. One man knew somebody who had seen cossacks riding through London on their wiry ponies, wearing fur hats and carrying the wickedly long lances for which they were famous. Another man said his friend had counted the Russians as they past and made the total 250,000 men. A third person said he knew a railway cleaner who swore that after the Russians left the trains at King's Cross there had been piles of snow left behind by their boots.

As the tales grew they became increasingly unbelievable. For a few weeks everyone believed the Russians had marched through London. But by late September nobody believed a word of it. Which leaves the intriguing question of what had really happened that dark night in August.

It seems almost certain that a large body of soldiers did arrive in London in the middle of the night, and was marched across the city perhaps to board trains heading south from Waterloo to a south coast port to be taken to France. The train timetables were severely overstretched at this time as huge numbers of men and equipment needed shifting in a hurry. The military had not yet gained control of rolling stock and timetables, so it is reasonable to assume that some trains were running at unusual hours.

That much of the story told by the porter, carter and watchman is reasonable enough. But what of the porter's statement that he did not understand the language the men spoke, and of the unidentified "man in a pub" who was told by an officer that the men were from Russia. Perhaps the porter was tired and muddled - by his own account he had just been rudely awakened from a nap. Perhaps "the man in the pub" never existed, or if he did he simply made up his story.

On the other hand it may be that the soldiers were not from Russia but from Ross-shire in the far north of Scotland. Delivered in a strong Scots accent the two words might not sound so different to a Londoner unaccustomed to talking to Scotsmen. And if the men were from Ross-shire, that might explain why the porter could not understand them. They may have been talking with impenetrable accents, or perhaps even in Gaelic - a language in wider use in 1914 than it is today.

Unfortunately for such neat theories, we know where the Seaforth Highlanders, the regiment recruited in Ross-shire, was in August 1914. The 1st Battalion was in India and did not return to Britain until December 1914. The 2nd Battalion was at Shorncliffe in Kent and had already gone to France when the mysterious men marched through London.

That the grim-faced silent men did march through London that night is certain. Who they were remains a mystery.

A German in Paris

On 17 August 1914 the Parisians woke up to find thousands of paper leaflets blowing around the boulevards and streets. The puzzled Parisians picked them up to look at them, and were at once both outraged and worried.

Each leaflet was printed in black on one side only. At the top was a savage-looking German Imperial Eagle. Underneath in large letters was written "People of Paris! The Germans are at your Gates. Tomorrow you will be ours!"

The police stations of Paris were soon overwhelmed with people bringing in handfuls of the leaflets. How had they got on to the streets? There was only one possible answer: Spies. The French capital must have German spies and saboteurs active and roaming the streets. The police agreed. By lunchtime it was clear that large areas of the city had been deluged with thousands of leaflets. The numbers of spies in the city must be enormous. Orders went out that that police were to stop and search anyone who looked either Germanic or suspicious.

Mayhem and confusion followed. Zealous policemen were soon rounding up dozens of people who had left their identity papers at home or who spoke with a funny accent. Police stations were soon bulging and the police were so busy checking up on the suspects that they had little time for anything else.

When the dust had settled, the French found that they had arrested no German spies at all. The search went on, but no German was ever found in Paris, and no more leaflets were ever distributed. How so many leaflets had been distributed over such a wide area of Paris in a single night remained a mystery to the French.

The Germans, of course, knew how they had done it. Or at least some Germans did, and that did not include the German High Command for it had been done without their knowledge or approval.

The men responsible were, in fact, two lieutenants in the German Air Force - Jacob Werner and Fritz von Hiddeson. On their own initiative they had the leaflets printed up and tied up in bundles. They then took off in their Taube monoplanes and flew to Paris as dawn broke. As they circled high over the city, they threw the leaflets out of the cockpits to flutter down to the city below. Aircraft were so new in the summer of 1914 that no Parisian thought to look up for a source of the leaflets, but assumed there must be a mass of Germans running about the streets.

The Missing Pilot

On 26 August 1914 Lieutenant Hubert Harvey-Kelley of the Royal Flying Corps was patrolling east of Le Cateau. His orders were to try to locate the bulk of the German army, then advancing to attack the British army in that town. Instead Harvey-Kelley flew into the history books.

While peering down to try to spot marching columns of men, Harvey-Kelley and his observer, Sergeant Major Street, instead saw a German Taube aircraft flying its own reconnaissance patrol. The British aircraft dived down as Street opened fire with a rifle, and Harvey-Kelley with a pistol. The two aircraft circled around each other, diving and climbing. Eventually one of the British airmen must have hit something, for the German's engine cut out and the Taube went into a dive.

The German aircraft landed in a field, and the two crewmen leapt out. They waved at the British aircraft, then ran off. Harvey-Kelley landed in the same field and strolled over to inspect the Taube. Knowing that he was well behind the advancing German armies, and not wanting the Taube to be useful to the enemy, he splashed some petrol over it and then set it on fire. The British then took off and returned to base.

Harvey-Kelley therefore became the first pilot to shoot down another aircraft. Unfortunately for the history books nobody knows the names of the German aircrew who were shot down.

Presumably they walked back to their base and reported what had happened, but if so it never got into any official German records.

Perhaps the Germans were not so keen to claim the distinction of being the first to be shot down as Harvey-Kelley was to gain the honour of being the first to do the shooting.

The Old Contemptibles

The British soldiers of the First World War who landed in France in August 1914 and took part in the long Retreat from Mons, later proudly referred to themselves as the "Old Contemptibles". It was a strange name, but one that was always spoken with pride and honour.

The phrase came about because of an order sent from Kaiser Wilhelm to General Alexander von Kluk, commander of the German First Army on 19 August 1914. The order was born out of the Kaiser's frustration at the way the war was going. The question is, did the Kaiser ever actually use the phrase ascribed to him.

Germany had gone to war determined to win a quick victory before her enemies could fully mobilise against her. The pre-war planning had been meticulous, but it was based on two assumptions of which both proved to be disastrously incorrect. The first assumption was that the vast Russian army would prove to be of a poor quality and would take about 10 weeks to mobilise and be ready for battle. The second assumption was that Britain would not join the war on the side of France.

The German plan for the war involved a clever division of German forces. A small force would be placed in East Prussia to deter, or at least slow down, any invasion by the small full time Russian army. It was hoped that this small force would be enough to keep the Russians at bay until the main Russian forces could be mobilised and brought forward. Meanwhile, in the west, the main German armies would sweep through Belgium, then turn south to outflank the French army and crush it in a war of annihilation. Once the French had been defeated, the Germans could move their armies east by rail to deal with Russia, which would by then be fully mobilised.

It was Chief of the General Staff, Alfred von Schlieffen, who in 1905 devised a plan to knock out France in six weeks, then turn on Russia. Schlieffen believed that France's first move would be to invade the provinces of Alsace and Lorraine which she had lost to Germany after defeat in the Franco-Prussian War of 1870. The strong German forts in the area would mean the French would have to commit most of their army to the advance. If the Germans then marched around the French flank and attacked them from behind, the French armies would be cut off from supplies and crushed between the German forts and German army.

The southern flank of the French armies in Alsace and Lorraine was protected by the neutral state of Switzerland and the high mountains of the Swiss Alps. The northern flank was protected by the neutral states of Belgium and Luxembourg. But Belgium was flat and had good roads that were ideal for marching columns of men and for the wagons that would keep them supplied. Von Schlieffen decided his armies would march through Belgium, even though this would involve invading a neutral country without warning. Von Schlieffen believed that once France was crushed, the Germans could evacuate Belgium with relatively little damage having been done. It would all be over before anyone could react.

As an introduction to his plan, von Schlieffen wrote:

"A battle of annihilation can be carried out today

according to the same plan devised by Hannibal in long forgotten times. The enemy front is not the goal of the principal attack. The mass of the troops and the reserves should not be concentrated against the enemy front; the essential is that the flanks be crushed. The wings should not be sought at the advanced points of the front but rather along the entire depth and extension of the enemy formation. The annihilation is completed through an attack against the enemy's rear... To bring about a decisive and annihilating victory requires an attack against the front and against one or both flanks..."

The plan depended on speed. Germany had to mobilise her armies within a couple of days, then the armies had to be moved up to the frontier quickly, then they had to march quickly, brushing aside whatever resistance the French could put in their way. Speed was everything. As soon as von Schlieffen's plan was approved by the Kaiser the General Staff was put to work. Railways heading to the Belgian border were given extra tracks and stations were enlarged. Arms were stockpiled and mobilisation plans revised to allow the German army to take to the field more quickly. Supply systems were modernised and upgraded so that they could keep up with the advancing columns.

Von Schlieffen retired in 1906 and was replaced by Helmuth von Moltke. He studied the plans and decided to alter them slightly. Von Moltke worried that the far right wing of the advancing German forces had a very long distance to march. It would leave Germany, march across Belgium entering France at Lille and continue southwest to Dieppe before turning south to Evreux and Chartres to surround Paris and thus cut off the French government from its armies in Alsace-Lorraine.

Von Moltke was certain that his men could march that far in the time allowed, but he was unconvinced that the supply system was up to the job of keeping them fed and their ammunition pouches filled. He was also convinced that if the French were able to mount an organised counter attack it would be against the centre of the advancing German front, perhaps near Laon. He therefore moved two corps from the right wing and put them in the centre. This meant the supply system had less work to do and gave the centre more power to roll over the anticipated French counterattack.

When the war broke out the French did exactly as the Germans expected them to do - they invaded Alsace and Lorraine. Von Moltke then threw his forces forward into Belgium and began the long march to surround Paris and attack the main French armies from the rear. Which was when things began to go wrong.

On 17 August the Russians invaded East Prussia, some 8 weeks before the Germans had believed they would be capable of doing so. The German I Corps halted the Russian advance at Stalluponen, but was then forced to retreat when more Russian units appeared on their flank. On 20 August Mackensen's XVII Corps was defeated at Gumbinnen. It was a small scale affair, but the German commander in the east, Maximilian von Prittwitz, took fright and ordered his entire command to fall back to the River Vistula to form a defensive line to stop the Russian advance on Berlin. That meant abandoning vast swathes of East Prussia. The Kaiser was furious.

Prittwitz was sacked and replaced by Paul von Hindenburg. At the same time three infantry corps and a cavalry division were taken from the western front and loaded on to trains to go East. That weakened the advancing German army in Belgium still further.

It was at this point that the Kaiser and von Moltke hurriedly debated revised plans for the west.

Not only had the German offensive been weakened, but the

defence had been strengthened. The British had unexpectedly joined the war and sent an army of 80,000 men to help the French. Arriving through the Channel ports it made most sense to place the British Expeditionary Force (BEF) on the left flank of the French defence, facing the right wing of the advancing German hordes.

In 1914 the far right wing of the German advance was made up of the First Army under Alexander von Kluck. On von Kluck's left flank was the Second Army under Karl von Bulow. The Kaiser issued a string of revised orders to his army commanders between 19 and 24 August. These were drafted by von Moltke, with the Kaiser usually signing them unaltered, though he always discussed them with von Moltke and occasionally suggested amendments. During this period the Kaiser also chatted to senior army officers, to his government ministers and to senior noblemen.

On 24 September the Orders of the Day for the BEF included - alongside routine supply instructions and troop movements - the following item:

> *'The following is a copy of Orders issued by the German Emperor on August 19th':*
>
> *"It is my Royal. and Imperial command that you concentrate your energies for the immediate present upon one single purpose, and that is that you address all your skill and all the valour of my soldiers to exterminate first, the treacherous English, walk over General French's contemptible little army. . . . " (HEADQUARTERS, Aix-La-Chapelle, August 19th.")*
>
> *"The results of the order were the operations commencing with Mons, and the advance of the seemingly overwhelming masses against us. The answer of the British Army on the subject of extermination has already been given."*

The item was picked up by the Press back in Britain and widely publicised. Government ministers referred to it, and the phrase "contemptible little army" was used time and again in recruitment drives. Cartoons appeared in numerous publications. Punch Magazine printed a cartoon of an injured and bandaged German Imperial Eagle speaking to the Kaiser. The Eagle is saying "Well, it's like this. You told me the British Lion was contemptible and, well, he wasn't."

The British army in France, meanwhile, had performed the grindingly exhausting Retreat from Mons, halted on the River Marne and together with the French halted the German advance. The British had taken heavy casualties, and would take many more over the months to come. When the men heard of the Kaiser's words they accepted the insult as a badge of honour and began calling themselves "The Contemptibles". The phrase stuck, though in newspapers as time passed it became "The Old Contemptibles".

The phrase came to refer to those soldiers who had gone to France when the war first broke out and who had fought at Mons or the Marne. The last surviving "Old Contemptible" proved to be Albert Anderson, who died aged 109 in 2005.

That the Kaiser had referred to the BEF as "a contemptible little army" was firmly believed by everone on the Allied side throughout the war. After all, in the context of the time, an order to roll over the British and continue on to Paris was exactly what the Kaiser would have told von Kluck to do.

When the German archives were opened up after the end of the war, the Kaiser's orders to von Kluck were revealed. They did indeed tell him to drive forward vigorously with his First Army to surround Paris, but they made no mention of the British at all. Von Kluck was told which towns to march through, which roads to use and how to supply his men, but the British were not so much as referred to, never mind called "contemptible".

The only reference to the British at about this time took the form of a telegram sent by von Moltke to von Kluck on 20 August which read "Disembarkation of English at Boulogne must be reckoned with. The opinion here, however, is that large disembarkations have not yet taken place."

Investigations were made of the officers who in 1914 had been drafting the Orders of the Day for the BEF. None of them recalled who had written the story, nor if they had ever actually seen captured German orders at the time.

A British officer who had been at Mons in 1914 and proudly counted himself an "Old Contemptible" was Sir Frederick Maurice who had ended the war as a general. He decided to investigate, using his status as military adviser to the Daily Chronicle newspaper to open doors. He got in touch with German newspapers to see if they had any reference to the phrase. Several did, but they all were in the form of articles quoting the phrase in the British press. None of them were direct quotes from the Kaiser and none predated October 1914, when the story was big news in the British media.

Maurice next contacted several German nobles and senior officers who had been in contact with the Kaiser in 1914. One of them remembered talking to the Kaiser during the German advance into France. He had asked the Kaiser if the presence of the BEF was a concern. He thought the Kaiser had replied with words to the effect that "Yes, it is a factor. But they should not hold us up for long as they are only a small army."

Maurice then used intermediaries to make contact with the former Kaiser himself, then living in exile in the Netherlands. The Kaiser was asked if he had used the phrase "contemptible little army". The exiled ruler was indignant. "Of course not," he snapped back. "On the contrary, I continually emphasized the high value of the British Army, and often, indeed, in peace-time gave warning against underestimating it."

Unable to get any further, Maurice gave up. He speculated that the phrase may have come from a captured German order or message of some kind passing between German commanders of individual divisions or corps and had been wrongly ascribed to the Kaiser. On the other hand, Maurice averred, it would not be the first time that an over-enthusiastic officer at General Head Quarters had made something up.

And so the source of perhaps the most memorable phrase ever to come out of the First World War remains an utter mystery.

The Crew of the Emden

THE GERMAN CRUISER SMS EMDEN was not in Germany when the war broke out, but in the Pacific. She at once embarked on a remarkable cruise of raids, battles and destruction which proved to be a mere curtain raiser to the mystery of what happened to a large section of her crew.

In 1899 Germany had taken over the Chinese port of Tsingtao, agreeing a 99 years lease that would allow them to use the port as a naval base in the Pacific. At this date Germany owned several islands in the Pacific - such as the the Marianas, the Caroline Islands and Samoa - and a good quality, deep water port was considered essential for a naval squadron that could guard them in times of war.

When war broke out in 1914, Tsingtao was home to the German East Asia Squadron. This consisted of the armored cruisers Scharnhorst and Gneisenau, plus the light cruisers Nürnberg, Leipzig, Emden and Dresden. The fleet also included eight small gunboats and the torpedo boat S-90. The German commander, Admiral Count Maximilien von Spee, followed the unfolding events of the July Crisis in Europe with keen interest.

On 3 August all the telegraph wires in and out of Tsingtao suddenly went dead. Von Spee knew that the telegraph wires were maintained by British companies and concluded, rightly, that Britain must be at war with Germany. He sent the cruiser Nurnberg to Hawaii to get definite news from the neutral USA, and meanwhile took his squadron to Samoa.

Having got firm news that war had been declared, von Spee considered his options. The combined forces of Russia, Britain and France in the Pacific vastly outnumbered his own ships.

Von Spee's last orders from Berlin had been to put to sea and harras Allied merchant shipping in the Pacific and Indian Oceans, while seeking to avoid a battle with naval forces. Such orders were all right as far as they went, but recently the British had given the Australian navy a brand new ship. The heavy battlecruiser HMAS Australia with its eight 12 inch guns might be able to defeat von Spee's entire force by itself. Australia was in Sydney when war broke out, but von Spee guessed she would soon be on her way to Tsingtao. He concluded that his original orders were now impossible to carry out. He decided to steam back to Germany. Nevertheless, he had to do his best.

Von Spee dispersed his fleet. The small gunboats were to stay around Tsingtao, evading capture as best they could. The bigger ships were to attack any merchant ships they saw, flee from any naval ships and to rendezvous at Easter Island to recoal for the journey back to Germany. That voyage began well with the Battle of Coronel on 1 November when the Germans met a small British squadron and sank two armoured cruisers. Disaster followed on 8 December at the Battle of the Falkland Islands where six of the eight German ships were sunk, and the other two were later captured.

Meanwhile the cruiser Emden had been at sea in the Indian Ocean. Following her existing orders to harry enemy shipping, Captain Karl von Muller went to work. With ten 4 inch guns and two torpedo tubes the Emden would be no match for large warships, but she was fast and easily powerful enough to sink merchant ships at will. Muller rigged up a false funnel and made other changes to the shape of his ship to disguise her and headed for India.

The Emden proved to be a highly effective raider, sinking or capturing 24 ships. Muller scrupulously observed the rules of war. Although he stopped several neutral ships, he sank them only if he found they were carrying war goods for the Allies. On 23 September Emden steamed into the port of Madras and opened fire. Two huge oil tanks went up in flames, a merchant ship was sunk and the dock facilities were badly damaged. Emden escaped unharmed.

The British put every warship to sea to find the Emden, and confined all merchant ships to port.

On 29 October the Emden steamed into Penang, a harbour in the British colony of Malaya. A joint Russo-French squadron was in port, but this did not deter Muller. The Russian cruiser Zhemdhug was in port, but Emden sank her with torpedos and then sank the French destroyer Mousquet badly damaged another as well as crippling the old French cruiser D'Iberville.

The Penang Raid persuaded the British to stop all convoys of food from leaving Australia for Britain until they could be guaranteed a powerful escort of warships. Muller was doing the German war effort much good, but it could not last.

On 9 November Muller attacked the British coaling station on the Cocos Islands, but the powerful HMAS Australia was nearby. She steamed to the rescue and inflicted such damage on Emden that Muller was forced to beach his ship and surrender.

It was while questioning prisoners that the Australians discovered that the Emden's first officer was ashore with a 53 man raiding party. By the time the Australians landed there was no sign of the Germans, but it was soon realised that a derelict schooner named the Ayesha was missing. Presuming that the Germans had absconded in the run down Ayesha, the Australians set out in search. They radioed far and wide an alert for the schooner, causing dozens of ships to start scouring the eastern Indian Ocean for the ship. For months the search went on. Nothing was ever found. It was concluded that the leaky old tub must has sunk in a squall. The Germans were written off as being dead, their fate was left a mystery.

In fact, Lieutenant Helmuth von Mucke and his men were very much alive. On leaving the scene of the action between Emden and Australia, Mucke had soon realised that the schooner he had stolen was leaking and unseaworthy. He put into an isolated cove and set his men to work carrying out repairs. Once the schooner was vaguely ready to go to sea, Mucke set sail for the Dutch East Indies (now Indonesia).

The Netherlands was neutral in the war, but Mucke knew that if he and his men were identified they would be interred for the rest of the war. Mucke therefore stayed away from the Dutch. He landed a man near the port of Padang on Sumatra and told him to visit the port and find out if any Germans were about. He found a German merchant ship, the Choising, which was earning a living sailing from port to port around the Indian Ocean taking whatever cargoes the captain could find. A meeting between the Choising and Ayesha was arranged at sea.

The captain of the Choising met Mucke and agreed to transport the German seamen to the nearest Ottoman port in the western Indian Ocean. At this date the Ottomans were allies of Germany and ruled extensive territories that today comprise Syria, Lebanon, Iraq, Kuwait, Saudi Arabia, Jordan and Israel. Much of this territory was controlled through local rulers who owed allegiance to the Ottomans but who had considerable freedom of action within their borders.

Mucke and his men were dropped off at Hudaydah, then in

Ottoman hands but now in the Yemen. The local Ottoman governor welcomed the Germans with open arms and asked how he could help. Mucke explained that he and his men wanted to go to the Ottoman capital of Constantinople so that they could get back to Germany. The governor agreed and gave Mucke and his men a house to live in while arrangements were made. After a while the governor summoned Mucke and explained that travel was difficult due to brigands. Payments would have to be made. Did Mucke have any money? On being told that the seamen had no money at all, the governor asked Mucke to sign a bill of exchange that could be cashed in with the German ambassador in Constantinople. Nothing much continued to happen, except the governor made repeated demands for money and bills of exchange.

After several months, Mucke decided that he was getting nowhere. He made contact with an Arab merchant who said he traded with the city of Medina, the southern terminal of the Hejaz Railway that ran north to Constantinople. For a sum of money he could get Mucke and his men to Medina by way of the port of Jeddah. Another bill of exchange changed hands.

The merchant took Mucke and his men down to the harbour and loaded them on to a number of sailing dhows, which then put to sea and headed north. They had not gone far when one of the dhows ran on to a coral reef off Zufaf Island. The crews became agitated and refused to carry the Germans any further. Wary of returning to Hudaydah, Mucke had himself and his men put ashore. They began the long walk up the coast to Jeddah.

The Germans had nearly reached the holy city when hundreds of horsemen were seen approaching. Mucke formed his men into a defensive ring and waited. As the horsemen got closer they turned out to be Bedouin tribesmen, who quickly opened fire on the Germans. The resulting battle cost the lives of one German officer and two sailors.

After some three days of desultory shooting, another force of horsemen was seen approaching. This turned out to be an army led by Hussein bin Ali, Sharif of Mecca. The Bedouin fled as the Meccan army approached. Mucke found a British rifle on the body of one of his attackers and concluded that the Bedouin must have been in the pay of the British, who controlled Egypt at this date.

Hussein bin Ali took the Germans to Jeddah, where he treated them as honoured guests. Once again the days and weeks dragged by with Mucke getting plenty of promises of help and support, but no actual action. One of the German sailors could speak Arabic and was tasked with purchasing food from the market. He came back one day to report a rumour that Hussein bin Ali was in secret talks with a British agent from Egypt with a view to launching a revolt that would gain him control of all Arabia and freedom from Constantinople. The tale was only a rumour but events would prove it to be true as Hussein bin Ali did rise in revolt a few months later.

Quickly concluding that he and his men were being held as hostages in the diplomatic game around the revolt, Mucke decided to flee. He sent his Arabic-speaking crewman to the harbour to talk to the dhow captains. One was found willing to take the Germans further up the coast in return for a bill of exchange. That night the dhow slipped out of harbour and a couple of days later Mucke stepped ashore at the little fishing port of Al Wajh.

At Al Wajh the head of the local Al-Bedaiwi tribe again welcomed Mucke and his men warmly with promises of support and help. Unexpectedly they turned out to be true. Mucke was given a guide and camels to carry his men inland to the Hejaz Railway. When the next train came along, Mucke flagged it down and demanded a ride. The German sailors were soon sitting in freight cars as the train trundled north.

Eventually in May 1915 Mucke and his men reached Constantinople. A telegram was sent to Berlin announcing their arrival. The German government trumpeted their escape from the British navy world wide. When Mucke got back to Germany he wrote up his adventures in book form and was then sent to the USA to publicise the book, and the German cause. He married an American of German extraction and returned to Germany a hero.

The mystery of the missing German crewmembers had been solved.

Saving Private Hitler

One of the mysteries of the First World War that did not surface until 1938, though the incident is said to have happened on 28 October 1914.

In 1937 Adolf Hitler, Nazi dictator of Germany, went to visit the home of a member of his staff, Dr Otto Schwend. During the visit, Schwend invited Hitler to see a painting that he had just received from a British friend, Lieutenant Colonel Earle. Earle and Schwend had met during the war when Earle was a prisoner and had remained in touch.

The painting showed an incident in September 1918 when British soldier Henry Tandey won a Victoria Cross carrying wounded men out of a field swept by German machine gun fire. The painting was a copy of the original by the famous Italian artist Fortunino Matania. Hitler took a close interest in the painting, particularly the figure of Henry Tandey. He asked for a photo of the painting to be sent to him, which Schwend did. Hitler had the photo framed and put on his desk.

In the autumn of 1938 British Prime Minister Neville

Chamberlain visited Hitler, at his mountain retreat at the Berghof for talks that would lead to the 1938 Munich Agreement. Chamberlain was surprised to see on Hitler's desk a photo of a painting showing British soldiers in action in the First World War.

Chamberlain asked about the picture. Hitler smiled, pointed to the central figure in the painting and declared "That man came so near to killing me that I thought I should never see Germany again; Providence saved me from such devilishly accurate fire as those English boys were aiming at us". Hitler then called an aide who was sent off to retrieve a scrap book, that turned out to contain cuttings from newspapers relating to Hitler's service in the German army during the First World War. Among the various cuttings was one relating to a British soldier winning a Victoria Cross. Hitler explained that he had kept the cutting because he knew the man, Henry Tandey.

Back in October 1914, Hitler recounted, he had been advancing with his regiment to attack the British when they came under heavy fire. Hitler was wounded and decided to go back to the rear for medical treatment. As he crept away, he glanced over his shoulder to see a British soldier aiming his rifle directly at him. Hitler froze, waiting for the shot to come. It never did.

The British soldier lowered his rifle and allowed the wounded Hitler to go on his way. Hitler said that when he saw the newspaper article about Tandey he recognised him instantly and linked his mercy to a wounded German in 1914 to his heroism saving the wounded in 1918. Hitler asked Chamberlain to pass on his kind regards to Tandey when he got back to Britain, then the meeting returned to affairs of state.

When Chamberlain got back to Britain, he sent a member of staff to find Tandey. The retired sergeant was by then working for the Triumph Motor Company in Coventry. Chamberlain sent a note to Tandey passing on Hitler's best wishes. The story soon leaked out and was reported in the press.

A reporter from the Coventry Herald went to see Tandey and interviewed him about the incident. Somewhat embarrassingly Tandey did not remember a thing about it. He admitted he never shot wounded, unarmed or retreating Germans, but did everything he could to kill them in battle. "Did I see Hitler?," Tandey responded, "I had the sights of my rifle on most of their gun crews, but whether I hit any of them I shall never know. I've wondered since how near I came to knocking down the future dictator."

Once war broke out between Britain and Germany again in 1939, Tandey became understandably reluctant to talk about how he may have saved Hitler's life. On the other hand he may have done no such thing. Perhaps it was somebody quite different who had failed to shoot Hitler on that autumn day in 1914. We will probably never know.

The Christmas Truce

THE STORY OF THE CHRISTMAS TRUCE is one of the best known of the First World War. The facts are well known and, now, well established, but this was not always so.

Censorship in 1914 was strict and little news got out to the public that the British government did not want to get out. The war was not going as well as had been hoped. Of all those involved in the decision to take Britain to war, only the veteran Lord Kitchener had rightly predicted that the war would not be over by Christmas but would, instead, last about four years. According to the plans the British and French armies should have been fighting a war of sweeping movement, driving the

German armies back to Berlin while the Russians advanced from the east. Instead the armies were stuck in cold, muddy trenches in France.

Of course, men home on leave could not be censored in the same way. They talked to friends and to family about their own experiences. And among those experiences for some of them was the Christmas Truce. Like the stories of the Angel of Mons and the Officer with the Drum, it became widely known at home and was reported in various newspapers - usually in the form of a story told by an anonymous soldier home on leave.

Officialdom, however, denied the story. Fraternising with the enemy was frowned upon, even at Christmas, and the story soon vanished from the headlines. By the 1920s it had been largely forgotten about, appearing in no regimental histories and glossed over and downplayed in every official account. In the 1930s one eminent historian wrote:

"That Christmas of 1914 will always be remembered for the preposterous tale of German-British fraternisation between the lines. It is a story that writers have revived in form or another over the years. It is interesting to note that few actual facts are ever offered, and that the incident is usually credited to some fictitious unit such as the Wessex Regiment. Anyone who ever served in the trenches will question that this holiday party took place. The author was not in France at this time, but in conversation with men who were in the British lines that Christmas, not one encountered any evidence of the incident."

We now know different, but it is an interesting light on how the truth can be misunderstood.

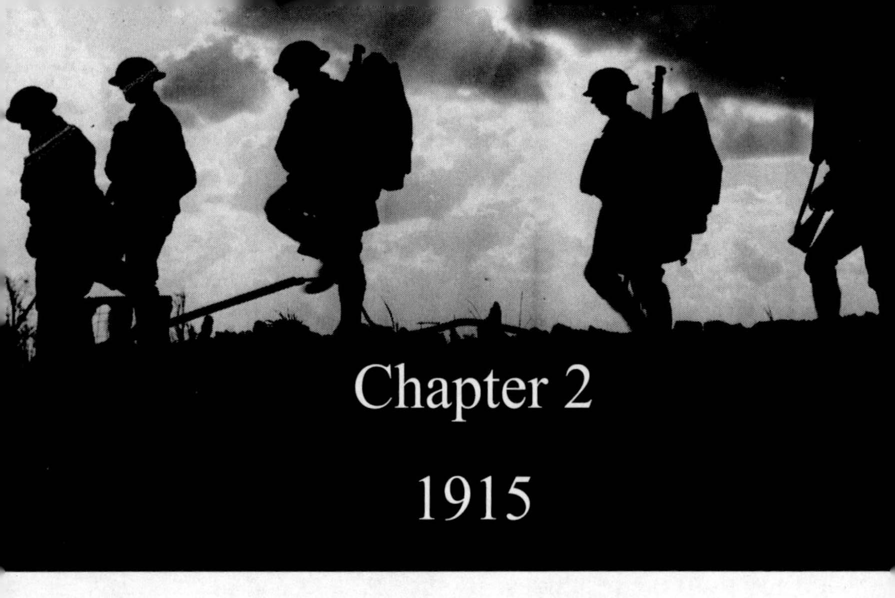

Chapter 2

1915

The Madonna of Albert

THE SMALL TOWN OF ALBERT in Picardy began life as a Roman fort in 54bc, and for the following centuries had led a largely blameless existence. The 19th century brought industrialisation and with it a prosperity the town had not previously known.

In 1885 the city fathers decided to spend some of that wealth on a grand new church for the town. They hired the noted architect Edmond Duthoit who produced for them the handsome Basilica of Notre-Dame de Brebières in a neo-Byzantine style. The soaring tower was topped by a statue of the Madonna herself, holding in her arms the baby Jesus. The statue was of metal and the city was proud of its lavish gilding.

In 1914 Albert had the misfortune to lie in the path of the fighting and it ended the year only a couple of miles behind the British front lines. Most citizens abandoned the town, going to live with friends or relatives, and the buildings were taken over by the British army. The mighty basilica, being a Catholic church, was treated as a place of interest by the largely Protestant British soldiers. A cafe was opened in the grounds.

On 15 January 1915 a stray German artillery shell coming down far from whatever it had been aimed at struck the tower of the basilica. The explosion tore away the brick cladding, but the internal steel structure - although badly damaged - did not give way. However the gilded statue of the Madonna was left leaning at a steep angle. As the months passed the occasional storm caused the statue to lean further and further. By the autumn she was leaning out horizontally from the tower, seeming to defy gravity.

The British Tommies who passed through Albert on their marches to and from the trenches as they went on and off front line duty used to gaze up at the crazily leaning Madonna of Albert. Far away the Germans could see the distinctive tower and bent statue. On both sides stories and legends grew up around the Madonna of Albert.

By 1917 the British soldiers were telling each other that the statue had been hit by the shell on the first day of the Battle of the Somme - that terrible day when so many men died or were injured. They also said that one day the Madonna would come to life, climb down from the tower and bring peace to the war stricken land and rest to the exhausted troops.

On the German side of the line the soldiers became convinced that whichever side knocked the Madonna from her perch would lose the war. The officers poured scorn on the idea, of course, but the men believed it. Albert was an important transport hub, with the roads leading in and out of the town being crucial to the British. From time to time the longer range German artillery were ordered to shell the roads. The firing was never effective. The men laying the guns always made sure their shells fell well clear of the Madonna of Albert, which meant they tended to miss the roads as well.

In March 1918 the Germans launched their last great offensive of the war. They smashed through the British lines and surged forward, overrunning Albert. Four weeks later, at the end of April, the Madonna came crashing down in the middle of a windy night to smash to pieces when it hit the ground. The Germans eyed the wreckage warily. Had they brought the Madonna down? Would they lose the war? The British pilots who flew overhead saw the statue had gone and predicted the war would soon end.

In fact the war dragged on to November, but it was the Germans who lost.

The Gurkha with a Silver Kukri

In March 1915 the first real British offensive of the war took place at Neuve Chapelle. The aim was to capture a ridge of high ground at Aubers, some five miles behind the German front lines. From that ridge the British artillery would be able to reach a strategic railway line that the Germans were using to supply all their armies in the Artois region. By cutting that line with artillery fire the British hoped either to force the Germans to retreat or to make them vulnerable to a major assault.

Responsibility for the attack was given to the British First Army, commanded by Douglas Haig. The French promised to launch a diversionary assault to the south to draw away German reserves a couple of days before the British attacked. Haig's preparations were careful and intense. In the weeks running up to the attack he had the Royal Flying Corps photograph from the air every inch of the German front lines and the territory it was hoped would be captured. From those photos detailed maps were drawn up with every German position marked. Careful plans were then developed on how to capture each German trench, strongpoint and emplacement. It was decided how many artillery shells would be dropped where and when, which troops should move forward at what time to capture what position and the timing for every move. Every officer was given a detailed map of his section of territory with clearly marked instructions as to what he and his men were expected to do.

On 10 March the plan was put into effect. The French had failed to carry out their part of the plan, but Haig remained confident he could take Aubers. At 7.35am the artillery opened up with the first phase of their planned bombardment. At 8.05am the whistles blew and the British infantry went over the top to sprint across No Man's Land to attack the German trenches. The attack was a complete success. The German front lines were captured, prisoners taken and the village of Neuve Chapelle secured. The first attacking units now paused, dug and began clearing the way for the reserves to pour through and surge on the Aubers Ridge before German reserves could arrive.

Then things began to go wrong. The fighting had smashed the land surface to chaotic mud scattered with broken pieces of barbed wire that snagged at trousers and slowed walking pace to a crawl. The telephone wires that each unit trailed behind itself as it advanced proved to snap easily, so most British units could not send messages back except by runner. The result was that the reserves did not learn for hours that the first attack had been successful. And once they did get moving their advance was agonisingly slow. Units supposed to go storming forward on the afternoon of 10 March were still moving up to their start positions at noon on 11 March. So great had been the weight of artillery fire on the first day, that many batteries did not have enough shells to open fire on the second day. By 12 March the British found that German reserves were in place and digging new trenches in front of Aubers.

It was at this point that the legend of the Gurkha with the Silver Kukri began. Haig suspected that the new German line at Aubers was too strong to break through, but wondered if the Germans had moved men from positions nearby, weakening them and making them vulnerable. He needed to know which German units were where, and that meant trench raids.

Trench raids were murderous night time assaults launched by small numbers of men. The aim was to approach an enemy trench unseen, slip in and kill or capture a few enemy soldiers. Once the enemy unit had been identified by regimental badges or shoulder flashes, the raiders withdrew - sometimes leaving behind booby traps to kill more of the enemy. Trench raids were not carried out only to identify enemy units, they often took place simply to keep the enemy guessing.

On the night of 13 March several trench raids were sent in around Neuve Chapelle and nearby areas. One such raid was carried out by a Gurkha unit attached to the Garwhal Brigade.

Among the patrol ordered forward was one man who had long excited the interest of his companions. This Gurkha did not mix with the other soldiers. Although he had joined as a simple private he spoke with an upper class accent and was clearly far better educated than the average Gurkha peasant. Rumours about him abounded and his fellows had finally concluded - on no evidence whatsoever - that he was the son of some rich and noble family who had somehow brought disgrace and shame to his family. Now he had joined the army to try to gain redemption through courage in battle.

Another thing that was odd about this man was his kukri. The Gurkhas carry into battle a large curved knife with a razor sharp blade on the inside of the curve. Most Gurkhas carried the kukri issued to them by the army, a functional but plain weapon. But this Gurkha had brought his own weapon. It was a beautiful work of art with a hilt of pure silver inlaid with gold wire and semi-precious stones. Few of the men could take their eyes off the weapon. They speculated if the blade was of as high a quality as the hilt. Was it a superb killing tool, or a pretty bauble better suited to noble dining tables than to the rough and tumble of battle.

When they were told that they were to go into action, the Gurkhas got their answer. Their mysterious comrade pulled out his kukri and began to sharpen it. The blade was awesome indeed, beautiful, gleaming and horrifically keen. As the Gurkha slipped his silver kukri back into its sheath he grinned wickedly and peered toward the German lines.

The Gurkhas were led by a British sergeant of the old Indian Army who explained exactly what they were to do. With the aid of a map and aerial photographs he pointed out the section of trench they were to raid, told the Gurkhas that they were to kill silently, retrieve regimental badges and stay close to himself. When he blew his whistle they were to muster to him and then dash back to the British trenches.

The men crept out of the British trenches around 1am. Working on hands and knees, freezing still whenever a star shell went up, the men crept across No Man's Land and through the barbed wire to the German trenches. They gathered around the sergeant who made sure everyone was present before giving the signal to go to work.

First into the German trench was the Gurkha with the silver kukri. He pulled out his knife and had slit the throats of the two Germans within sight before the sergeant's boots hit the floor of the trench. While one man cut the badges off the corpses, the sergeant sent one group of men one way and led another himself. At his side strode the man with the silver knife, moving as silently as a moon shadow along the trench. A German dozing in a fire step was killed while he slept. When a dug out entrance appeared, the Gurkha dashed down to massacre the five men within. The sergeant was impressed and unnerved in equal measure.

Deciding that he had enough German badges for the task in hand, the sergeant signalled that his men should return to where they had first entered the German trench. The Gurkha shook his head, smiled and slipped around a corner in the trench. An ominous silence followed. When the sergeant peered around the corner he saw another German corpse slumped on the trench floor - but there was no sign of the Gurkha. After waiting as long as he dared, the sergeant led his other men back the way they had come.

The sergeant blew his whistle to summon back his men. Within a couple of minutes everyone was gathered together, except the Gurkha with the silver kukri. The sergeant blew his whistle again. A German star shell went up. It was time to go. After one last look around, the sergeant scrambled out of the trench and led his men slowly back to their own lines.

The raid had been a complete success, with only one casualty. The Gurkha with the silver kukri was missing.

Six days later and four miles up the line a British sentry heard something moving in No Man's Land. Thinking a German patrol was out cutting the British barbed wire ready for an attack, the soldier summoned his sergeant. The sergeant also heard the sounds of movement and put together a squad to go out and confront the German patrol. The men clambered out of the trench as quietly as they could and squirmed forwards. The sounds of movement had stopped, but the British still moved forward, though more warily than before. Then they found the German patrol - three men all dead with throats expertly slit.

A few days later in another section of the line another trench raid was carried out by a British patrol. They had no specific mission in mind, intending only to test German vigilance. They crept forwards, gaining the German lines with ease. The men dropped down into the German trench and found two German soldiers slumped against the trench wall. Thinking the men were asleep, the soldiers lunged to try to take them prisoner. But the men were not asleep, they were dead. Both of them had had their throats expertly cut by some weapon of frightening sharpness.

Every now and then over the following weeks British soldiers on patrol or on a raid would find German soldiers lying dead with their throats cut. It was not long before somebody put two and two together, linking the missing Gurkha to the dead Germans. Clearly the mysterious Gurhka with the silver kukri was on the move, killing Germans whenever he could. Whatever private disgrace he had brought to his family had surely been more than avenged.

This tale of the Gurkha with a silver kukri on a killing spree was a well known one to British soldiers, with everyone convinced it was true. However, the story has been reported in various different forms by different men. The event has been located on the Somme in 1916 and at Ypres in 1917 as well other places. The essentials of the story remain constant - that an enigmatic Gurkha with a beautiful silver kukri went on a trench raid, then embarked on a murderous campaign of slaughter that was tracked by the British soldiers in that section of the line by the corpses of the Germans he killed.

The version given above which locates the event at Neuve Chapelle in 1915 is the earliest known, so perhaps this is the true and original. The Gurkhas are known to have fought in this action, though whether the Gurkha with the silver kukri ever really existed is far from clear.

BURLINGTON BERTIE

AT SOME TIME IN THE SPRING OF 1915 - nobody was ever certain when - British soldiers manning the lines a little north of Ypres came to be aware of a highly colourful figure whom they quickly knew as "Burlington Bertie", a reference to a popular music hall song of the time. The true identity of the man has never been firmly pinned down.

At this date both sides sent up giant balloons that soared over the battlefield, tethered to the ground by strong steel cables. Under the balloon dangled a wicker basket in which stood a man equipped with binoculars and a telephone. His task was to watch where artillery shells fell, then telephone the battery to give them advice on how to correct the fall of shot so as to hit whatever they had been aiming at.

Understandably the other side did not take kindly to the presence of balloons and did their best to destroy them. Given that the balloons were filled with highly flammable hydrogen this was none too difficult. All that needed to be done was for an aircraft to attack using guns firing incendiary bullets, and even a few hits would result in the balloon falling in flames. The balloons were soon accompanied by anti-aircraft guns, but the best defence against attack was to winch the balloons back down to earth. The hapless observer in the basket, meanwhile, would usually leap from the basket to float back to earth using his parachute. The same balloon might go up and down a dozen times a day as aircraft threatened an attack, then veered away.

The mysterious Burlington Bertie was one of the British observers who went up in the balloons. It was said up and down the line that this particular officer had begun training to be a pilot in the RFC, but for one reason or another had earned the ire of his seniors and had been sent to sit in a balloon instead of fly an aircraft. Now, every morning as he went out to clamber into his basket the would-be pilot appeared in a top hat, plum-coloured velvet smoking jacket and ornate walking stick. The ground crew of the balloon met him with a good-natured chorus of "Burlington Bertie from Bow", to which the balloonist responded with ornate flourishes of hat and stick before being sent aloft.

The song described a poor East End young man who would dawdle about in fashionable West End streets pretending to be a rich young idler, while all the time being too poor even to afford a decent meal. The chorus went:

I dress up in fashion
And when I am feeling depressed
I shave from my cuff all the whiskers and fluff
Stick my hat on and toddle up West
I'm Burlington Bertie I rise at ten-thirty
and saunter along like a toff
I walk down the Strand with my gloves on my hand
Then I walk down again with them off
I'm all airs and graces, correct easy paces
So long without food so long, I've forgot where my face is
I'm Bert, Bert, I haven't a shirt
But my people are well off you know.
Nearly everyone knows me from Smith to Lord Rosebr'y,
I'm Burlington Bertie from Bow.

If a German aircraft came near, the ground crew would begin lowering the balloon while Burlington Bertie took to his parachute. Ordinary mortals would simply jump and open the parachute, but not Burlington Bertie. Instead he put on a show, pretending to be walking on thin air as if strolling down some fashionable street in London and doffing his hat to passing ladies. Only then would he open his parachute and land safely.

It was this performance that the men in the trenches would see. They responded with cheers and their own rendition of the music hall song, belting out the words with joyous cheer.

Burlington Bertie was moved up and down the line along with his balloon as the needs arose. Wherever he went he cheered up the troops on the ground with his comical show. He is mentioned in dozens of letters home by infantry in the trenches, so he most certainly did exist. But who he was remains a total mystery for the records of the balloon corps make no mention of the man and his - no doubt entirely unofficial - antics.

The Crucified Canadian

ONE OF THE MORE MACABRE MYSTERIES of the First World War relates to an incident which is thought to have occurred in the spring of 1915 near Ypres. The story has gone in and out of fashion over the years, being firmly believed in for some time, then dismissed as a fabrication for a few years before another historian declares it was true all along.

The story began circulating among soldiers in France in April 1915. As with other such stories that were repeated as true incidents, the different accounts varied in detail, though the essentials remained the same. The basic story was that the Germans had launched an attack against a Canadian regiment somewhere near Ypres in early 1915. The assault had been initially successful and the Canadians had been pushed back, but then a counterattack had taken place and the Germans had been driven back again. As the Canadians drove the Germans back they naturally came across the bodies of men killed in the fighting, and wounded. One of the dead men was a Canadian soldier whose body had been fixed to a barn door or other wooden structure by German bayonets. In most versions the body was said to have been crucified, with the body held in place by bayonets thrust through the hands and feet as if the man had been crucified. Versions differed as to whether the man had been alive or dead when he was bayonetted to the door.

It should be explained to readers accustomed to thinking of First World War battlefields as blasted wastelands of mud swept clear of everything except death and destruction that in the spring of 1915 the battlefields were very different. The rival armies had only recently settled down into their trenches and the artillery had not yet had time to pound to destruction all buildings, trees and roads in the area. In several areas abandoned villages stood intact in No Man's Land, so it was very possible that a barn had changed hands in the fighting.

In any case, the story first surfaced outside France in the pages of the Times newspaper. The story was short and written by a reporter in Paris. The reporter got the story from a group of wounded soldiers in hospital, who had heard it from the Dublin Fusiliers who, they said, had seen the incident themselves. The times said the victim had been a Canadian officer, that he had been alive when pinned to the "wooden farm building" and that the Germans had then killed him.

Sir Robert Houston, MP for Liverpool West, must have then spoken to his contacts in the military for a few days later he asked a question in the House of Commons of Harold Tennant Under-Secretary of State for War. The quesion was "whether he has any information regarding the crucifixion of three Canadian soldiers recently captured by the Germans, who nailed them with bayonets to the side of a wooden structure?"

Tennant replied that he did not. Houston responded by asking if Tennant was unaware that several Canadian soldiers had signed affadavits in front of the British officer commanding the military base at Boulogne, and what was the War Office intending to do about it. Clearly caught on the hop, Tennant said that he would look into the matter.

On 15 May a letter from an anonymous soldier appeared in the Times stating that the victim was a sergeant and had been fixed to a fence not a door. Letters from anonymous servicemen were common at this date. The newspapers were generally aware of who the writer was, but kept the name back to avoid repercussions for the man from his comrades. Censorship was, however, strict so details of military operations and movements were not generally discussed or printed unless approved by the War Office.

Four days later Houston asked about the matter in Parliament again. Tennant replied that investigations were under way and that he could not comment further until the investigations were complete. Those investigations were being conducted by Colonel Ernest J. Chambers, a Canadian staff officer. He diligently visited units around Ypres trying to find an eyewitness to the event.

Eventually he found a Canadian who claimed to have seen the body. The tale he told was not exactly as it had been reported. The event had happened at St Julien on 24 April as the Canadians attacked to recapture ground lost to the Germans two days earlier. He said that he had found three Canadian soldiers who appeared to have been bayonetted to death while wounded and helpless. One of the bodies had been propped up against a barn door and held in place by a bayonet through his body. The dead man had been named Brant, but no other details were available.

The tale was bad enough, but lacked the gruesome details and religious overtones of the original story. Believing he had got to the bottom of things, Chambers filed a report and moved on.

The story, however, refused to die. It was repeated up and down the line by soldiers, featured in magazines and formed the basis of incidents in several fictional war stories and movies. The celebrated British artist Francis Wood created a stunning 32 inch tall bronze sculpture of the incident that he entitled "Canada's Golgotha". After the war the German government asked the Canadians either to provide proof the incident had happened or to remove it from an official war exhibition. After some prevarication the sculpture was removed, though it later formed part of another exhibition entitled "Under the Sign of the Cross: Creative Expressions of Christianity in Canada".

By the 1930s the story had been largely forgotten, and those who remembered it generally thought it was untrue. But in 2004 documentary film maker Iain Overton looked into the story. He found some letters and other documents relating to the Central Ontario Regiment of the Canadian Infantry. These made it clear that the event had really happened. The victim had been Sergeant Harry Band. His body had been pinned to a barn door by eight bayonets and there were signs that he had been killed by the Germans when a wounded prisoner.

At the time his comrades had sought to cover up the truth as they knew that Band's family would have been deeply distressed by the horrific facts. The story had leaked out as troops gossiped to each other, but the men steadfastly refused to confirm to reporters what had really happened or the name of the victim. The story told to Chambers was the closest that outsiders ever got to the truth.

The Lost Norfolks

IN AUGUST 1915 TWO BATTALIONS of the Norfolk Regiment were taking part in the arduous Gallipoli Campaign. The campaign had begun as a naval dash up the Dardenelles to reach and bombard Constantinople, thus forcing Turkey to make peace. The naval ships were held up by coastal forts at Gallipoli, so troops were landed to capture the forts and open the way for the ships.

Soon the campaign got bogged down in the sort of trench warfare that dominated the Western Front. The British forces were largely composed of the Australian and New Zealand Army Corps (ANZAC), with some British support. The Turks were well dug in, well led and supplied with all the guns and ammunition they could want, while British and Anzac supplies had to be hauled the length of the Mediterranean. To make things worse for the British, Gallipoli was very hot in summer, with temperatures soaring under a blazing sun, and there were no natural sources of water in the pockets of land occupied by the invaders.

It was into this nightmare campaign that the 1/4th and 1/5th battalions of the Norfolk Regiment marched, straight from the recruiting grounds of Norfolk. They formed part of 163rd Brigade of the 54th Division.

In August the British commander, Sir Ian Hamilton, decided to launch a renewed assault on the Turkish positions. The 1/5th Norfolks were detailed to carry out a preliminary operation on the later afternoon of 12 August. They were to advance into some wooded hills near Kavak Tepe to clear out Turkish snipers who were located in the woods and could dominate the British line of advance.

The 1/5th Norfolks were supposed to advance at 4pm following a brief, but intense 45 minute artillery bombardment. As was frustratingly common in Gallipoli under Hamilton, things went wrong before they even started. The 1/5th Norfolks were told not to advance until 5pm, but the artillery were not informed of the change. They laid down their bombardment, then ceased fire. An hour later, by which time the Turks had had plenty of time to prepare for the attack, the Norfolks advanced. They met with determined and heavy resistance.

Hamilton's official report back to London described what happened next:

"In the course of the fight, creditable in all respects to the 163rd Brigade, there happened a very mysterious thing. Against the unyielding forces of the enemy, Colonel Sir H Beauchamp, a bold, self-confident officer, eagerly pressed forward, followed by the best part of the battalion. The fighting grew hotter and the ground became more wooded and broken. At this stage many men were wounded or grew exhausted with thirst. These found their way back to camp during the night. But the Colonel with 16 officers and 250 men still kept pushing forward, driving the enemy before him. Nothing more was seen or heard of any of them. They charged into the forest and were lost to sight or sound. Not one of them ever came back."

The fate of the 1/5th Norfolks proved to be an enduring mystery. For the rest of the Gallipoli campaign it became a talking point up and down the lines. Some decidedly odd theories were put forward, but nothing could ever be said for certain. When Turkey eventually surrendered in 1918 the British assumed that prisoners from the 1/5th would clear up the mystery. There were none in Turkish prisoner of war camps. The Turks denied they had ever captured the 1/5th and said they knew nothing about the men.

The mystery deepened. It was only going to get stranger.

On the 50th anniversary of the Gallipoli landings many veterans went to Gallipoli to pay tribute to their fallen comrades in the war cemeteries. The subject of the Lost Norfolks came up again, and three New Zealanders volunteered a most peculiar story. Having kept quiet for fear of ridicule they now spoke up.

Sapper F. Reichardt, Sapper R Newnes and JI Newman told their story, then wrote it down and signed an affadavit before going home. Their story ran as follows:

"The following is an account of the strange incident that happened on the 21 August 1915, which occurred in the morning during the severest and final period of fighting which took place on Hill 60, Suvla Bay, Anzac.

"The day broke clear, without a cloud in sight, as any beautiful Mediterranean day could be expected to be. . The exception, however, was a number of perhaps six or eight 'loaf of bread' shaped clouds - all shaped exactly alike - which were hovering over Hill 60. It was noticed that, in spite of a four or five mile an hour breeze from the south, these clouds did not alter their position in any shape or form, nor did they drift away under the influence of the breeze. They were hovering at an elevation of about 60 degrees as seen from our observation point 500 feet up. Also stationary and resting on the ground right underneath this group of clouds was a similar cloud in shape measuring 800 feet in length, 220 feet in height and 200 feet in width. This cloud was absolutely dense, solid looking in structure and positioned about 14 to 18 chains from the fighting in British held territory. All this was observed by 22 men of No.3 Section, No.1 Field Company NZE, including myself from our trenches on Rhododendron Spur approximately 2,500 yards south west of the cloud on the ground. Our vantage point was overlooking Hill 60 by about 300 feet. As it turned out later, this singular cloud was straddling a dry creek bed or sunken road and we had a perfect view of the cloud's sides and ends as it rested on the ground. Its colour was a light grey, as was the colour of the other clouds.

"A British regiment, the 1/4th Norfolk, of several hundred men, was then noticed marching up this sunken road or creek towards Hill 60. However, when they arrived at this cloud they marched straight into it with no hesitation but no one ever came out to deploy and fight at Hill 60. About an hour later after the last of the file had disappeared into it, this cloud very unobtrusively lifted off the ground and, like any cloud or fog would, rose slowly until it joined the other similar clouds which were mentioned at the beginning of this account. On viewing them again, they all looked alike as peas in a pod. All this time the group of clouds had been hovering in the same place, but as soon as the singular cloud had risen to their level they all moved away northwards towards Thrace. In a matter of about three quarters of an hour they had all disappeared from view.

"The regiment mentioned was posted as missing or wiped out and on Turkey surrendering in 1918, the first thing Britain demanded of Turkey was the return of this regiment. Turkey replied that she had neither captured this regiment nor made contact with it and did not know it existed. A British Regiment in 1914-1918 consisted of any number between 800 and 4000 men. Those who observed this incident vouch for the fact that Turkey never captured that regiment, nor made contact with it.

"We, the undersigned, although late in time, this is the 50th jubilee of the Anzac landing, declare that the above described incident is true in every word."

The account circulated among veterans for a while, adding to the mystery rather than solving it. The tale was then picked up by UFO enthusiasts and hit the headlines. An entire British regiment, it was said, had been kidnapped by aliens in a UFO. It was a sensational claim that made what was already a baffling mystery even more bizarre.

And yet, the account by the New Zealanders was written 50 years after the event. Human memory is a notoriously frail thing and over such a period of time mistakes and errors can, with the best will in the world, occur.

Some of these errors are immediately obvious in the account. The New Zealanders said they saw the 1/4th Norfolks vanish on 21 August, but it was the 1/5th Norfolks who went missing on 12 August. Other errors require a bit more research to uncover. The New Zealanders said that they saw the British disappear close to Hill 60 at a distance of 2,500 yards from where they were standing on Rhododendron Ridge. In fact Hill 60 is nearly 7 miles from Rhododendron Ridge. Moreover, the 1/5th Norfolks did not vanish attacking Hill 60 but some wooded hills a couple of miles away.

For years the story of the alien abduction of a British regiment did the rounds. Those keen on seeking to prove the reality of aliens in UFOs accepted it, others rejected it. Finally in the 1980s some detailed research into the affair threw up an explanation.

On 21 August an attack did take place on Hill 60 that went wrong because of fog. The attack by the Sherwood Foresters had been timed for early evening, when the setting sun should have been full in the faces of the defending Turks. That would have hampered the fire of the defenders, while the clear Mediterranean air would have allowed the Australian artillery to see the Turkish positions and lay down accurate fire.

In the event an unseasonal fog came down as the sun dipped toward the horizon. This meant the Australian gunners could not see the Turks, while the Turks could see the advancing infantry very clearly indeed. The attack began, but was quickly called off when it was realised that to continue was suicidal. The men went to ground to evade the rifle and machine gun fire from the Turkish trenches, then retreated when night fell.

It would seem that this is what Reichardt, Newnes and Newman watched from the top of Rhododendron Ridge. They would have seen a British regiment march into a mist. When the mist lifted the men were nowhere to be seen, having taken cover to avoid the Turkish fire. Presumably over the intervening 50 years the three New Zealanders had muddled their experience on 21 August with the disappearance of the Norfolks on 12 August. Mixing up two peculiar events is an easy enough mistake to make given the passing of the years.

That, of course, leaves the fate of the Norfolks still a mystery. The answer to the mystery is not certain, but there are enough clues to put forward a rather disturbing suggestion.

There was one prisoner in Turkish hands from the 1/5th Norfolks who had been captured on 12 August. This was Private Arthur Webber. He had been injured by a shot to the head early in the advance. The battalion advanced on as Webber slipped in and out of consciousness. After a while he heard men walking toward him, then a shot, followed by another. Webber moved his head and saw a Turkish soldier lift his rifle and shoot dead a wounded British soldier as he lay on the ground. Webber feared his own death was imminent, but at that moment a German officer came running up. Webber passed out again and came to in a Turkish hospital. He was convinced that he owed his life to the German who he presumed must have stopped the Turk shooting him dead.

Another clue came from a member of the War Graves Commission, Rev Edwards, who in 1919 heard from a Turkish farmer of a mass grave. The Turk said that when he came back to his farm following the evacuation of Gallipoli by the British-Anzac force he had found a number of dead British bodies on his land. Not sure what to do with them, he had pushed them into a ravine and thrown earth over them. The farm was not far from where the 1/5th Norfolks had vanished. It was presumed that these bodies were those of the missing men. The Rev Edwards had the bodies dug and moved to a proper cemetery, though there was nothing to firmly identify the individual bodies.

Putting the two accounts together the most likely explanation is that the 1/5th Norfolks ran into superior Turkish forces. They may have fought to the last man, or they may have sought to surrender but the Turks did not prisoners that day. They shot everyone, even the wounded. Only Webber survived to tell his harrowing tale. If that is what happened the mystery would seem to have been solved, but in truth nothing about this incident is certain.

The Secret Cargo of the Lusitania

At sea the war had started with a flurry of activity. German warships in distant lands had preyed on Allied merchant ships for months, but had eventually either been hunted down or simply run out of coal. Closer to Europe the Battle of Dogger Bank saw a German cruiser sunk and a British battlecruiser crippled. Fast German warships steamed across the North Sea to bombard British harbours at Hartlepool, Yarmouth and elsewhere while smaller ships fought coastal battles in the Channel.

The rules of war at sea had been drawn up before the advent of radio, and this had a profound effect on how the war was fought. Unarmed merchant ships were supposed to be given time for the crew to take to lifeboats before they were either captured or sunk. However, with radios the merchant crew could send out an alert that would bring naval warships hurrying to the scene. This was a deterrence to the Germans when attacking merchant ships.

The use of radios was particularly difficult for U-boats. These submarines attacked warships without warning by firing torpedoes from below the surface. They were supposed to attack merchant ships by surfacing, giving the crew time to escape and then sinking the ship with gunfire. But with merchant ships now sending out radio signals to summon help, the U-boat was then very vulnerable to counter attack when a warship hastened to the rescue.

On 4 February the German navy issued the following statement that was sent for publication in all neutral states:

> *"(1) The waters around Great Britain and Ireland, including the whole of the English Channel, are hereby declared to be a War Zone. From February 18 onwards every enemy merchant vessel encountered in this zone will be destroyed, nor will it always be possible to avert the danger thereby threatened to the crew and passengers.*
>
> *"(2) Neutral vessels also will run a risk in the War Zone, because in view of the hazards of sea warfare and the British authorization of January 31 of the misuse of neutral flags, it may not always be possible to prevent attacks on enemy ships from harming neutral ships."*

The statement was accompanied by a map for mariners showing the area that the Germans were declaring to be a war zone.

Almost at once the U-boats began attacking merchant ships with torpedoes without warning. The deck guns were also used, but only when the U-boat commander was confident that no Allied warships were close enough to intervene. The number of ships being sunk rose dramatically, as did the death toll among civilians.

Despite the dangers, ships continued to steam for Britain. Travelling by ship was the only way for people or goods to get across the seas. The war demanded that Britain import not only the usual amount of food and raw materials, but also huge quantities of munitions. And war or no war people needed to travel on business or for other reasons. In any case the vast majority of ships got through without difficulty and the British navy was patrolling the seas with destroyers and laying minefields off the German U-boat bases.

In an effort to hamstring the Allied merchant marine the German Embassy in America placed the following advert in American newspapers:

"NOTICE!

TRAVELLERS intending to embark on the Atlantic voyage are reminded that a state of war exists between Germany and her allies and Great Britain and her allies; that the zone of war includes the waters adjacent to the British Isles; that, in accordance with formal notice given by the Imperial German Government, vessels flying the flag of Great Britain, or any of her allies, are liable to destruction in those waters and that travellers sailing in the war zone on the ships of Great Britain or her allies do so at their own risk.

IMPERIAL GERMAN EMBASSY
Washington, D.C. 22 April 1915"

By chance one American newspaper printed the warning next to a Cunard advert for the trans Atlantic liner RMS Lusitania. It was a coincidence that would become famous.

On 1 May 1915 the Lusitania left New York for Liverpool. She was a fast ship and was taking precautiions against U-boats. Once the ship got into the war zone night lights were doused and the ship followed a zig-zag course that was designed to make it much more difficult to hit the ship with a torpedo. The interior watertight doors were all shut, lifeboats prepared to be launched and double lookouts put on duty. In the event, it was all to no avail.

At 1.25pm Captain Walther Schwieger of U-20 sighted a large ship approaching and prepared to attack, but the ship turned away and Schwieger assumed his craft had been seen. He set a course for home, but then the large ship turned back toward the U-boat. Schwieger recognised the ship as a large passenger liner. As the Lusitania raced at top speed toward the U-boat, Schwieger fired one torpedo.

On board Lusitania lookout Leslie Morton saw the torpedo and shouted a warning, but there was not enough time for the ship to turn out of the way. The torpedo hit the starboard side adjacent to the bridge. There was the expected explosion as the weapon hit. A few seconds later there was a second and much larger explosion which has never been explained.

The ship began to list quickly, the great speed of the ship causing the inrushing water to burst the watertight bulkheads and increase the speed of sinking. The heavy list and continuing forward speed seriously hampered the crew as they tried to launch the lifeboats. Most lifeboats were capsized or took on water as they were launched from the ship, which within three minutes had a 15 degree list. A few minutes later the bows dipped under the waves and then hit the muddy bottom that lay just 300 feet below the surface. Just 18 minutes after the torpedo hit the Lusitania had gone down. Many people had gone down with her, hundreds more were in the water.

Fishing boats nearby raced to the rescue, as did other ships once they realised what had happened. Even so the death toll was frightful. Of the 1,959 people on board, 1,195 had died.

There was an immediate and powerful international reaction to the sinking. The destruction of merchant ships without warning had caused protests, but most accepted that the Germans had a right to sink such ships, and understood the reasons for the U-boats attacking without surfacing. But the sinking of a passenger liner without warning was another matter entirely. Most people in neutral countries could not accept that a passenger liner was a legitimate target of war in the first place, and the sinking without warning was seen as a clear breach of the rules of war.

Outrage in the USA was especially strong as 128 of the 139 US citizens on board had died. President Wilson sent a string of strongly worded protests to the Kaiser. As a result the Germans declared that they would no longer attack passenger liners at all while merchant ships from neutral states would no longer be attacked without warning. Instead neutral ships would be stopped and searched. If they were found to be carrying war supplies to Britain they would be sunk, otherwise they would be set free. Only British or French ships would be sunk without warning.

Meanwhile, the German navy refused to accept it had done anything wrong. They declared that the ship had been carrying munitions, that she was armed with a gun and that the Royal Navy was using her as an Armed Merchant Cruiser (AMC). The British at first denied all this, but it quickly emerged that Lusitania did have on board 4,200 cases of rifle ammunition, 1,250 artillery shell cases and 18 boxes of fuses. The fact that under international rules, none of this was classed as war supplies did nothing to quell German claims that the ship had been carrying munitions.

It was also quickly clear that the Lusitania was on the reserve list of AMCs held by the Royal Navy. The task of these merchant ships was to assist warships in guarding a convoy. They tended to be faster merchant ships and were fitted with guns or depthcharges. The Lusitania had been fitted with mountings for guns, but no weapons had actually been fitted.

In the event the fuss eventually blew over, but it was never forgotten. In 1917 the Germans resumed unrestricted U-boat warfare. Soon afterwards the USA declared war on Germany.

Meanwhile there were questions about the sinking that would not go away. Prominent among these was the second and larger explosion that had followed the torpedo strike. Those on board Lusitania assumed that a second torpedo had been heartlessly fired by the U-boat even though the liner was already sinking. The Germans insisted that only one torpedo had been fired. They assumed that the second blast had been caused by explosives that they said the Lusitania must have been carrying.

In the USA other questions were being asked. At the official inquiry, Captain Turner of the Lusitania refused to address certain issues on grounds of wartime secrecy. This was not good enough for the Americans. They wanted to know:

Why the Lusitania had reduced her speed, even though she was in a war zone.

Why the Royal Navy had not sent a destroyer escort, even though destroyers were available.

Why Lusitania was not warned that a U-boat was known to be in the area

What exactly was on board the Lusitania.

Adding to unease in the USA was suspicion among some that Britain was very keen indeed for the USA to join the war against Germany. It was not only German-Americans who believed that the British had over exaggerated stories of German atrocities in Belgium and elsewhere. Now there was a suspicion that the British were again up to no good. Some even thought that the British had deliberately sent the Lusitania into danger in the hope that a large number of American deaths would bring the USA into the war.

This allegation has never entirely gone away. An investigation in the 1990s by a journalist found that the signals sent between Lusitania and the navy during the 48 hours before the sinking were missing from the official files. No amount of searching was able to find them.

Another issue that was raised in the immediate aftermath was the question of what had been on board. Passenger liners carried cargo in their bowels, and it was known fairly quickly that some of that cargo had been rifle ammunition. A close study of the list of cargo revealed that a large American explosives factory had sent a large number of boxes, described as being "fur" and "butter" to a Royal Navy base in Essex. There was an immediate suspicion that the boxes marked fur and butter in fact contained explosives. It has since emerged that the boxes of butter were not put in the refrigerated part of the hold as they should have been if they really did contain butter. Both the American company and the Royal Navy refused point blank to answer any questions about the boxes.

Neither of these issues were adequately dealt with at the time, but given the vast slaughter taking place at the time they were slowly forgotten. Both issues were catapulted back into the public view in the early 1990s when improvements in diving gear meant that divers could easily get down the 300 feet to reach the wreck.

The first men to dive the Lusitania found that the ship was a mess. What should have been a largely intact hull was instead in pieces. The damage had clearly been caused by underwater explosions. Lying near the wreck was a British naval depth charge, clearly indicating what had caused the damage. "There's no doubt at all about it that the Royal Navy and the British government have taken very considerable steps over the years to try to prevent whatever can be found out about the Lusitania," announced one expert who viewed photographs of the damage.

The British government then began legal action in the Irish Courts claiming that the wreck was the property of the Royal Navy as the Lusitania had been an AMC at the time she sank. This would have made all recovery of objects illegal. After a two year case the judge ruled that the wreck did not belong to the Royal Navy as it lay inside Irish territorial waters and so it belonged to the Irish Navy instead. Inevitably the British action fuelled rumours that the British had something to hide.

What that something might be has never been discovered.

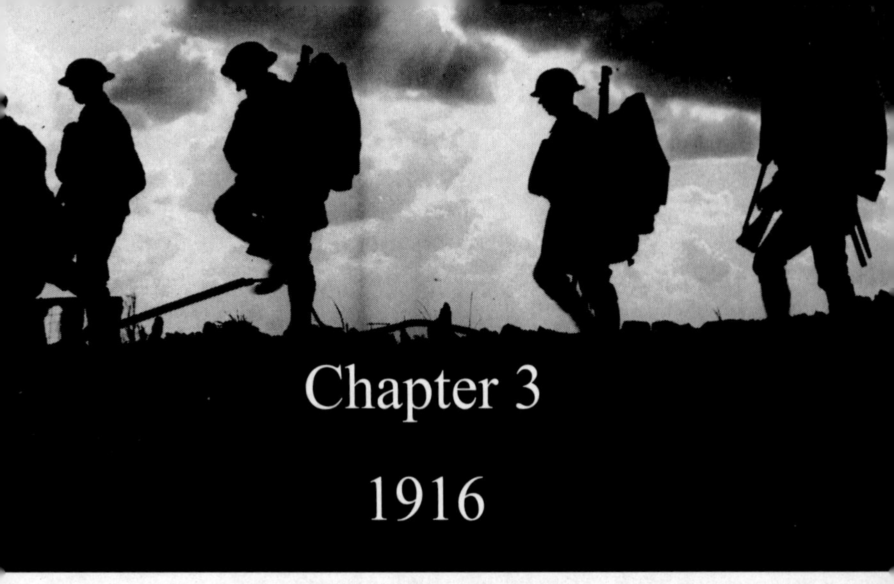

Chapter 3

1916

The Real Biggles

In 1932 a fictional pilot in the Royal Flying Corps first appeared in print in a short story called "The White Fokker". The pilot was named James Bigglesworth, but he has always been better known by his nickname of Biggles.

Although he later enjoyed a lengthy fictional career as a police pilot, charter pilot and fighter pilot in World War II, the vast majority of the Biggles stories put him firmly in the First World War. The stories were written out of chronological order, but a career for Biggles can be put together. He joined the Royal Flying Corps in the spring of 1916 and learned to fly that summer before joining an active squadron in September that year. At first Biggles flew two-seater observation aircraft but by the spring of 1917 he was in single-seater "scouts", later to be known as fighter aircraft.

Biggles had a vast number of thrilling adventures during the war. He shot down 32 German aircraft, was forced down himself eight times and was awarded the Military Cross and bar as well as the Distinguished Service Order. The early stories were written for adults, but Biggles soon attracted a younger readership so later stories were aimed more obviously at younger teenagers and some of the early stories were rewritten for the new audience.

The author of the stories was Captain William Earle Johns, who habitually wrote as W.E. Johns. Johns himself had gone to war as an infantry officer in 1915, transferring to the RFC in 1917. In September 1918 he was shot down and taken prisoner by the Germans. After the war Johns became a journalist specialising in aircraft related issues. He began writing the Biggles stories in between his more serious journalistic assignments, but very quickly took up Biggles full time as the popularity of the stories secured him a steady income.

Johns never made any secret of the fact that the stories were mostly fictionalised versions of real events that had happened to himself or his comrades during the fighting in the air during 1917 and 1918. However, Johns always maintained a veil of secrecy over which, if any, pilots had served as the models for the various characters that feature in the books. Most attention has focused on Biggles himself and who was the "Real Biggles".

An early favourite candidate was Albert Ball, the great pilot who not only notched up an impressive tally of enemy aircraft shot down but was also a popular officer among his comrades. Those who knew him said Ball had an engaging personality and sense of humour, but was single-mindedly devoted to shooting down enemy planes in the air - much as was Biggles at least in the earlier stories about him. However, Johns always said the stories were based on people and events that he had known in the RFC. Ball was killed in action several weeks before Johns joined the RFC, so that would seem to rule him out.

Another candidate is Arthur Bigsworth, whose name is suggestive of Bigglesworth. Bigsworth learned to fly in 1913 and as soon as the war broke out he joined the Royal Naval Air

Service. By 1916 he had attained the rank of Wing Commander and continued to have a distinguished flying career. After the war he decided to remain in the services and obtained a permanent commission with the newly formed Royal Air Force. By 1922 he was commanding the RAF throughout the Mediterranean while being based in Malta. In 1925 he returned to Britain and worked at the Air Ministry until his retirement in 1935. Johns met Bigsworth several times during these years and the two men seem to have got on well. Bigsworth rejoined the RAF when war broke out in 1939 but by this date was too old to fly. He spent the war commanding a number of maintenance and other non-combatant bases. He retired again in 1945 and died in 1961 at the age of 76.

In many ways, Bigsworth is not a close fit for Biggles. Despite the similar names he did not serve in the RFC, never flew over the Western Front and never shot down a German aircraft, though he did win the DSO when he bombed a German U-boat and sank it in the English Channel. On the other hand, Johns did know him reasonably well.

Another favourite to be the Real Biggles is Cyril Lowe. born in 1891, Lowe went up to Cambridge where he quickly shone as a star rugby player. While still at Cambridge he was called to play for England in 1913 and began piling up an impressive succession of high scores and spectacular tries. His haul of 8 tries in England's Grand Slam triumph of 1914 remains a record.

When war broke out, Lowe at once volunteered for the Royal Flying Corps and by 1915 was flying over the Western Front. In the summer of 1918 Lowe, like Biggles, won the DSO. His citation reads:

"This officer has destroyed five enemy machines and driven down two others out of control. On one occasion he attacked two enemy triplanes, although at the time only one of his guns was serviceable; he shot down one of the machines in flames.

On another occasion, while leading a formation of eight scouts he engaged a hostile formation of twenty-six machines. Having shot down a Fokker biplane he went to the assistance of one of our scouts and drove the enemy machine down to 500 feet; at this low altitude half of a blade of his propeller was shot off by fire from the ground. Supplement to the London Gazette, 3 August 1918."

A few weeks later he, again like Biggles, was awarded the Military Cross, the citation reading:

"For conspicuous gallantry and devotion to duty. This officer and another pilot were escorting a formation of machines engaged on a bombing raid when seven enemy scouts attacked the bombers. They both attacked these scouts, but at the outset this officer's machine was set on fire, and the other pilot's right hand top plane broke. During the fight that ensued each came to the rescue of the other. The other pilot first caused Capt. Lowe's pursuer to break off his attack, and then Capt. Lowe shot down the scout attacking his comrade. The action of both these officers, in practically unmanoeuvrable machines, in coming to the rescue of each other in turn, showed courage and self-sacrifice of a very high order. Supplement to the London Gazette, 16 September 1918."

Unlike Biggles he did not win a bar to the MC. He ended the war with 9 confirmed kills, compared to Biggles's 32.

After the war, Lowe left the services and resumed his rugby career. Despite having had his sporting career interrupted by the war, Lowe achieved a number of records. His total of 18 tries for England remained unsurpassed until 1989. He is not known to have met Johns

Also suggested was William "Bull" Statton. Statton joined the famous Artists Rifles in 1915, moving to the RFC in 1917. He went to the Western Front as a fighter pilot in the spring of 1918. He achieved fame on 26 March when he shot down three

German aircraft in a single day and quickly became first a flight leader and then a squadron leader. He had shot down 26 German aircraft when he was badly wounded by an exploding bullet on 24 September and forced out of the war. He had by then been awarded the DSO, MC and DFC and bar.

Between the wars Statton remained in the RAF, transferring to fly bombers. He was still flying bombers when World War II broke out. He was one of the first to try to solve the accuracy problems of bombing at night by using flares.When that proved a success he started experimenting with a number of other techniques that would later become standard in the RAF and would inspire the formation of the Pathfinder Force. He then transferred to the Far East where he was captured by the Japanese and subjected to horrific tortures, the results of which remained with him for the rest of his life. After the war he gained the rank of Air Vice Marshal before he retired in 1952. He died at home at the age of 94.

Statton knew Johns, though not very well, and his personal character would seem to have been similar to that of the fictional Biggles.

The mystery seemed to have been finally solved in 2013 when a Daily Mail reporter came across references in the RAF archives to a "James Bigglesworth" who had left the RAF in 1920 to join a rather shadowy organisation linked to MI5. The reference made it clear that MI5 wanted the war record of this James Bigglesworth to be removed from the RAF records for "operational reasons" linked to his new role in the secret services. In particular MI5 were keen to remove all references to a specific patrol over Hazebrouke in August 1918.

Rather unfortunately the story turned out to be an April Fool's Joke perpetrated by a reporter who had read the Biggles books as teenager.

The mystery of the Real Biggles remains.

Something Wrong with our Bloody Ships

AFTER NEARLY TWO YEARS OF SKIRMISHES, circling each other and minor battles the two greatest war fleets afloat finally faced each other in a two day battle from 31 May to 1 June 1916 when the German Imperial Navy's High Sea's Fleet and the Royal Navy's Grand Fleet met off the west coast of Denmark in what became known as the Battle of Jutland. The day would go badly for the British, for reasons that nobody could understand.

The decision of the Germans to build a powerful war fleet to protect German merchant shipping and help build a colonial empire had been one of the key factors that led to British-German hostility after 1904 and has been blamed as one of the main reason Britain joined the war.

It was, therefore, a prime war aim of the British to reduce and if possible destroy the German navy as an effective fighting force. By contrast the primary aim of the Germans was to keep their navy in being.

Earlier in the war the Germans had used fast ships to race across the North Sea, bombard British ports and then dash back to Germany before the British could respond. By 1916 the Germans were aware that the British had brought forward their own force of battlecruisers commanded by Vice-Admiral David Beatty and based them in the Firth of Forth.

German Admiral Reinhard Scheer planned to lure the British battlecruisers to their destruction. He would send his five battlecruisers, under Vice-Admiral Franz Hipper across the North Sea as if on a coastal raid. When Beatty and his nine battlecruisers came out, Hipper would retreat as if fleeing, but in reality would merely be luring Beatty toward the main German fleet that would be lurking over the horizon.

In 1916 there was a distinct and definite difference between "capital" ships intended to form the main strength of a war fleet fighting another war fleet and other ships intended to attack or escort merchant ships, guard ports and secure the sea lanes.

The prime capital ships were battleships. These behemoths displaced over 30,000 tons and were armed with 6 or 8 enormous guns with a calibre of 15 inches. They were protected by steel armour that was up to 13 inches thick on the gun turrets and 6 inches thick on the main deck. They were awesomely powerful warships, but they were relatively slow and had a limited range due to the heavy armour and the limited space available for coal.

The other type of capital ship was the battlecruiser. These ships were slightly smaller than the battleships, but just as heavily armed. They did, however, have lighter armour on the deck of about 3 inches. The battlecruisers were faster than battleships and had a longer range. Their job was to steam ahead and around the main force of battleships, using their superior speed and range to cover large areas of ocean and their big guns to sink or drive off enemy cruisers, destroyers and other small ships. Battlecruisers could also be used for independent missions, such as coastal raids or attacking convoys. They were not intended to face up to battleships due to their lighter armour.

Hipper went to sea in the early hours of 31 May and steamed north up the west coast of Denmark, a neutral state. He was followed by Scheer with the bulk of the German High Seas Fleet steaming a few hours behind him.

Meanwhile, British intercepts of German radio signals had revealed that the High Seas Fleet was putting to sea, though the details of the German plan were unknown. Beatty and his battlecruisers went to sea and steamed east. Behind Beatty came Admiral Sir John Jellicoe with the Grand Fleet.

Beaty and Hipper sighted each other at 2.20pm on 31 May, long before the Germans expected the clash to occur. As planned, Hipper turned as if retreating and Beatty followed him toward the German High Seas Fleet. It took until 3.50pm for the big battlecruisers to get within range of each other, when they opened fire.

Beatty had with him 6 battlecruisers, 13 cruisers and 18 destroyers. Not far behind him was the 5th Battle Squadron of Rear Admiral Hugh Evans-Thomas with 4 battleships and 10 destroyers. Hipper had five battlecruisers and four cruisers, plus a host of small, fast gunboats and torpedo boats. The advantage in terms of firepower lay with the British. However, Evans-Thomas missed several of Beatty's signals and so the British battleships ended up over the horizon and unable to join in the initial clashes.

The rival battlecruisers began trading salvoes of shells as the ships steamed south. At 4.02pm HMS Indefatigable was hit by three 11 inch shells fired by SMS Von der Tann, which knocked out a gun turret and smashed her steering. As Indefatigable fell out of the fighting formation, she was hit again. A terrific explosion tore the ship apart. A gun turret was hurled some 200 feet into the air as flames and smoke enveloped the entire ship. When the smoke cleared the ship had gone. A German torpedo boat dashed in to rescue survivors. Only two dazed men out of 1,019 men on board were found alive.

At 4.25pm HMS Queen Mary went the same way as Indefatigable. She suddenly exploded in a blinding flash of flame that blasted upwards beside the foremast. The ship snapped in two and went down like a stone. Of 1,266 men on board only 20 were picked up alive by the British destroyer HMS Tepperary that dashed to the rescue.

In the meantime Beatty's own flagship, HMS Lion, had taken several hits. A gun turret was put out of action and the ship was on fire.

Then a third battlecruiser, HMS Princess Royal, erupted in flame and smoke. Beatty turned to Captain Alfred Chatfield of the Lion who was standing next to him and said "There seems to be something wrong with our bloody ships today." The words would become famous, as would the way Beatty then turned toward the German ships to close the range.

When the smoke cleared it showed that Princess Royal was still afloat. One of her gun turrets was out of action and she was burning furiously, but she was still underway.

A few minutes later the main High Seas Fleet came into sight. Beatty now turned about in his turn as if fleeing, but in fact seeking to lure the German ships toward Jellicoe and the Grand Fleet.

At 6.21pm another British battlecruiser, HMS Invincible, exploded. Again a vast blast tore the ship into pieces, hurling large lumps of metal high into the air and deafening all those nearby. The ship broke in two and went down quickly, though due the shallow water, the two halfs remained standing upright and sticking out of the water for some hours. There were only six survivors and among the dead was Rear Admiral Horace Hood DSO.

As dusk closed the main war fleets sighted each other and began trading shots. But night was falling and accuracy was difficult. Several times during the night that followed the two fleets came close to each other and opened fire. By now Scheer was keen to get away. His plan to ambush the British battlecruisers had gone well, but he had no wish to tangle with the Grand Fleet. The night fighting was confused, but when dawn came it was clear that Scheer had got away.

Both sides claimed a victory. The British said they had swept the Germans from the sea and forced them to flee. The Germans pointed out they had sunk more British ships than they had lost themselves. The British had lost 3 battlecruisers, 3 cruisers and 8 destroyers. The Germans had lost 1 battlecruiser, 1 old battleship and 4 light cruisers.

Meanwhile, the British were left to puzzle over what had gone so tragically wrong with their battlecruisers.

The only real clue to the disaster was a photo taken of HMS Invincible as she exploded, This showed that the base of the blast was Q turret, one of two twin gun turrets mounting 12 inch guns that were located between the second and third turrets. One of the few survivors was Gunner Bryan Gasson, who had actually been inside Q turret when the blast occurred. He was closely questioned, but unsurprisingly could remember very little. He had been in the turret following orders one second, and floating in the sea the next. The handful of survivors from the other ships could add little. All they could recall was the blast of German shells hitting the ship, followed by a single monumental blast.

It was quickly apparent that the only possible source of such a titanic explosion would have been the ammunition stores of the ships themselves. No German shell could have exploded with such power. Yet the magazines were protected beneath the armoured deck and within steel walls that were not only blast proof but also fire proof.

Attention then shifted to the hoists which carried shells from the magazine to the gun turret. These had blast and fire proof doors at both top and bottom which, in theory, would stop any fire in the turret or close by from travelling down into the magazine and causing an explosion. Changes were made to the design of the magazines, the hoists and the turrets just in case these had been at fault.

The mystery of what happened was never properly solved.

The Death Flight

In September 1916 the German air ace Oswald Boelcke made a combat report that would prove to be one of the most enigmatic of the war.

Boelcke was leading Jagdstaffle 2 - the premier fighter squadron in German service - on a patrol near Marcoing. The squadron had recently been re-equipped with the brand new Albatros D.II fighter. Boelcke had set himself the task of using his three squadron unit to achieve complete control of the air over his section of the front line. He had hand picked his pilots from among the most promising men in the German air force, among them Baron Manfred von Richthoffen who would later earn fame as the Red Baron.

The flying conditions were good, with calm weather and scattered cloud. The patrol had been uneventful.

Boelcke was leading his staffel in a V formation toward a cloud bank when suddenly another aircraft erupted from the cloud flying straight at them. The German pilots had to scatter in desperation to avoid a collision. Boelcke recognised the machine as a British R.E.8 observer aircraft. Throwing his aircraft into a turning climb, Boelcke then dived down on to the rear of the British aircraft and fired his guns with his usual unerring aim.

Nothing happened. The British plane flew on east toward the German rear area as if nothing had happened. Puzzled, Boelcke threw his fighter in to a turn and was racing back to fire again when he saw Richthoffen flying alongside the British aircraft and waving vigorously. Boelcke too came alongside and his gaze followed his comrade's pointed finger.

The British pilot and observer were sitting bolt upright in their cockpits, both staring straight ahead. A smear of blood ran down the side of the R.E.8. Both men were clearly dead. The German pilots watched the British aircraft as it bored on east toward what had been the Belgian border before the war began. After a while, Boelcke dipped his wings in salute and led his patrol off back to their hunting grounds.

When he landed Boelcke wrote out his usual combat report, referring to the enigmatic British machine as carrying out a "Death Flight". Fairly soon the Death Flight was the talk in German squadron messes up and down the line. But there was a problem. No British aircraft had crashed anywhere near Marcoing, nor to the east. Not only that but it was soon clear, and confirmed after the war, that no R.E.8 squadrons had been operating in the area.

Where the British aircraft had come from and where it went to, nobody could ever explain.

A Dead Landing

On 9 December 1916 an R.E.8 aircraft belonging to an Australian unit within the Royal Flying Corps landed at the airbase near St Pol sur Mer. The aircraft was not based there, but few of the men watching it land were much surprised. Aircraft routinely landed at bases not their own if they ran short of fuel, got lost or merely fancied a chat with some one else for a change.

This particular aircraft came down for a perfect landing, trundled forwards toward the officers' mess and came to a stop. Everyone expected the two man crew to hop out and stroll over to join the St Pol officers, but nothing happened. When neither man on board had made an effort to get out for some minutes, one of the watching officers strolled over to investigate.

He found that both men in the aircraft were dead, riddled by

German bullets, the fuel tanks were empty and the throttle was wide open.

The men must have fallen victim to a German aircraft some miles away, with their engine flat out. The aircraft had then flown on until its fuel ran out, when it glided down to the ground and landed at St Pol.

Thc men at St Pol shook thier heads in amazement. They pulled the bodies out, found that the dead men were a Lieutenant Sandy and a Captain Hughes, then phoned their home squadron to come and collect the bodies for burial.

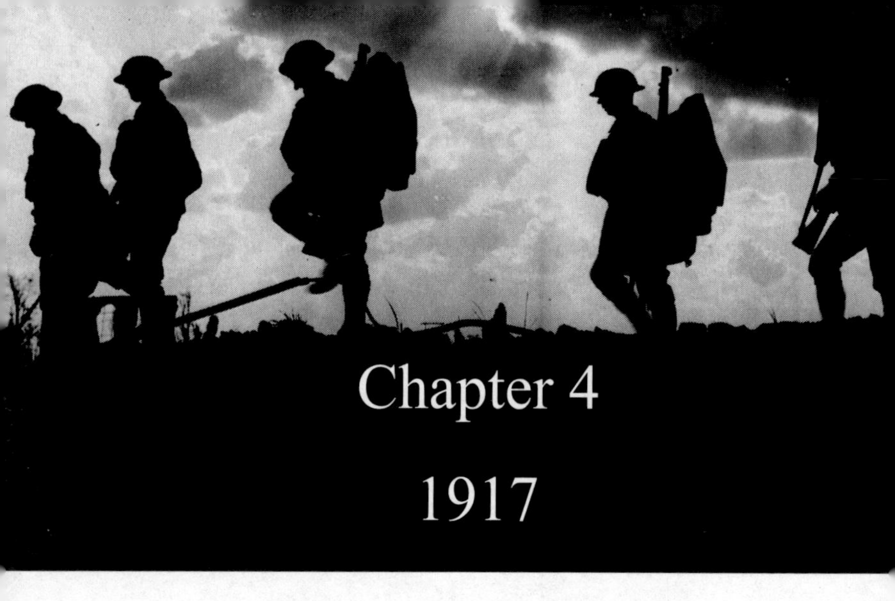

Chapter 4

1917

The Innocence of Mata Hari

In October 1917 the French government announced that the internationally famous - and infamous - dance star Mata Hari had been shot as a German spy. The outcry was immediate and loud. Mata Hari was a notorious sex symbol who had scandalised early 20th century society with her raunchy stage show, but the idea that she had been a spy seemed rather far fetched. More worryingly, she was Dutch and therefore a neutral national. Had the French been justified in shooting her? The French refused to say anything much, other than to insist that they were right.

Mata Hari had exploded on to European show business in 1905. She claimed to be from the Dutch East Indies, now Indonesia, and that she was an exiled Javanese princess of Hindu birth who had trained from birth in the secret arts of sacred dance. Her name was Indonesian for "Eye of the Day", or "Sun at Dawn". She was vague about the reasons for her exile, but dropped hints it had to do with a tragic love affair.

The stage act was, she said, an adaptation of the holy dances performed in secret in Hindu temples. Whatever its origins, it was scandalous, sensual and astonishingly popular. The dance involved Mata Hari gyrating around a stage decorated to look like an Indonesian temple in a series of sexually provocative dances. The climax came as she cast off her clothes until reduced to only a tiara and bra of silver gilt metalwork studied with jewels.

To further boost her earnings and notoriety, Mata Hari posed for a number of photographs in which she was virtually nude - then a quite astonishing thing to do - and gave newspaper interviews about her past, the East Indies and her hopes for the future. She mingled in the highest of society, flirting with every man she met and wearing the most daring of outfits for social occasions.

Her dancing was highly acclaimed by those in a position to know what they were talking about. There was a fashion at the time for avant garde choreographers to look to exotic cultures for inspiration. Isadora Duncan, for instance, favoured Egypt. Mata Hari may have earned notoriety for her lack of clothing, but the arts establishment were captivated by her Eastern influences and nimble footwork.

Very soon her act began to be imitated by others. Dancers of voluptuous figure but little talent realised that they could get bookings and high fees by pretending that their dances were also based on genuine Eastern culture, when in fact they simply involved the women taking their clothes off. Mata Hari's popularity began to suffer and her income declined.

Mata Hari then moved on to men as a source of money. She became the mistress of wealthy French industrialist Emile Guimet, but also had a string of other lovers. She seemed to develop a liking for socially and politically important men, and for men in uniform. She counted several politicians and senior officers among her conquests.

When war broke out, Mata Hari had to obtain a Dutch passport to be able to continue her travels, performances and love affairs. It turned out that the "Javanese princess" was really a Dutch woman named Margaretha Geertruida Zelle. Born in 1876, Zelle married a Dutch army officer of Scottish ancestry named Rudolf MacLeod when she was 18. The young couple moved to the East Indies when MacLeod was posted there and,

Mata Hari, photographed at the height of a her fame in one of her typically flamboyant "Javanese" costumes.

at first, were happy. They had two children and mixed with the highest society in the colony.

However, MacLeod later turned to drink and kept a local girl as a mistress. By 1903 he was an alcoholic and was suffering from syphylis. Zelle left him, adopted the name of Mata Hari and began her sensational stage act. When war broke out in 1914, Mata Hari continued with her careers as dancer and lover using her Dutch nationality to move freely around neutral and belligerent countries.

The way she mixed so freely with senior military officers, diplomats and government officials led to suspicion among the counter-espionage department at Scotland Yard in London. When she arrived in Britain from Spain in November 1916 she was arrested and taken in for questioning. She was interviewed by Sir Basil Thomson, one of Britain's most experienced interrogators. The interview was lengthy and during it Thomson managed to catch Mata Hari giving misleading answers to some questions. Thomson managed to corner Mata Hari and she eventually broke down and told him that she was a spy for the French and for the Belgians.

Thomson did not believe her. He thought that she was a flighty, silly woman who could no longer earn a living on the stage and was inventing a new role for herself while sponging money off whichever men she could lure into her bed. She was set free and went back to Spain.

In Madrid she began an affair with a good looking German diplomat named Kalle. In reality this diplomat was the head of German espionage in Spain. He ran a number of spies both in Spain and, by way of intermediaries, in France. Kalle paid some large sums of money to Mata Hari at this time. Early in 1917, Mata Hari travelled to France and was promptly arrested by the French.

The French had tracked Kalle's money to Mata Hari. They

had also intercepted a radio message sent by Kalle to Berlin in which he praised the work of "Spy H21", saying that H21 had handed over some very useful information in return for cash payments. The French put the two facts together and concluded that Mata Hari was H21. They investigated Mata Hari and turned up the succession of affairs with military men and diplomats that had alarmed the British.

At her trial, which was held in secret, Mata Hari treated the accusations with contempt. Of course she had taken money from Kalle, she said, how else was she supposed to live? Of course she had had affairs with rich and important men, what was she supposed to do, throw her beauty away on poor, ugly men? Did she talk about the war? She talked about whatever her lover wanted to talk about, what else? "My international connections are due of my work as a dancer, nothing else .... Because I really did not spy, it is terrible that I cannot defend myself" she wrote in protest at the ruling that neither she nor her lawyer would be allowed to question witnesses called by the prosecution. Indeed, much of the evidence against her was not shown to her, only to the judges.

It seems to have come as a complete surprise to her that the French thought she was a spy, and an even greater shock when she was found guilty and sentenced to death by firing squad.

She was shot on 15 October 1917. She wore a fashionable dress and refused a blindfold.

Disputes have raged ever since as to whether she was really a spy or not. The evidence that has emerged since 1917 has been complex, contradictory and confusing. In the Netherlands in 1914 she had taken a large sum of money from the German consul, Karl Kroemer. It may have been compensation for the loss of her luggage, impounded in Berlin when the war broke out. Or it may have been a recruitment fee for Kroemer was a spymaster. In 1916 she met Georges Ladoux, head of French military intelligence and more money passed hands. She may have been recruited as a French spy, or the money may have had some other reason.

It seems the mystery about Mata Hari must remain unsolved.

The Corpse Conversion Factory

On 17 April 1917 The Times newspaper printed a gruesome and appalling story. Apparently the German army was taking the bodies of battlefield casualties to a top secret "Kadaververwertungsanstalt" (Corpse Utilization Factory). There the bodies were boiled and rendered to produce fats, oils and other chemicals that could then be used to manufacture fertiliser, explosives, soap or candles.

It was a sickening story, but was it true?

The Times said that they had got the story from another newspaper, La Belgique. This was a newspaper printed by Belgian exiles in the Netherlands that was intended for both the local exiles and for clandestine distribution into occupied Belgium. When La Belgique was asked where they had got the story, they pointed to a German newspaper, the Berliner Lokal-Anzeiger. The German story was not actually about the Corpse Conversion Factory itself, but was a sort of travelogue written by a reporter visiting the Western Front and writing up his experiences. The relevant section about the Kadaververwertungsanstalt was quite short and read as follows:

"Next we pass through Evergnicourt. There is a dull smell in the air, as if lime were being burnt. We are passing the great Corpse Utilization Establishment (Kadaververwertungsanstalt) of this Army Group. The fat that is won here is turned into lubricating oils, and everything else is ground down in the bones mill into a powder, which is used for mixing with pigs' food and as manure."

By the time investigations had tracked the origins of the story down to this short passage, it had spread like wildfire. The French newspapers were full of it, and the Times account had been reprinted across the British Empire and in the USA. A week after the Times story first appeared the humorous magazine Punch printed a famous cartoon showing the Kaiser in typically heartless pose explaining to a recruit that a use could be found for him alive or dead.

The matter was raised in Parliament in the form of a question. The minister Robert Cecil replied that he had no information at all on the subject other than what he had read in the newspapers, then added "in view of other actions by German military authorities, there is nothing incredible in the present charge against them". Despite this the government's propaganda department did circulate copies of the Times article to newspapers in neutral countries and sought to get the story covered as widely as possible.

In May the story gained new credibility when an undoubtedly genuine German army order was captured in the front line and passed to the Times. It stated that carcasses should whenever possible be sent to a German army unit referred to as "VsdOK" to be passed on to the Kadaververwertungsanstalt. The Times was triumphant at being vindicated and declared that the VsdOK was an abbreviation for the Verordnungs-Stelle, or "Instructions Department".

Nothing further was ever heard of the Kadaververwertungsanstalt and its hideous works. No eyewitnesses came forward to say they had seen it, nor further German documents referred to it. Gradually the story faded from memory.

But not from everyone's memory. The Germans had not liked

the accusations and in 1925 they finally persuaded the British government to make an announcement. Sir Austen Chamberlain read out a statement in the House of Commons in which he explained that the VsdOK unit was in fact an abbreviation for the Veterinar-Station, or Central Veterinary Command of the German army. The carcasses that had been processed were those of the many hundreds of horses killed in the fighting, or that had died of disease.

And so the mystery of the hideous Kadaververwertungsanstalt was finally laid to rest.

The Ghost Plane of Calais

Throughout the First World War aircraft flew back and forth over the English Channel as replacements were sent out to France and existing aircraft came back for servicing. The pilots usually flew over the Channel at its narrowest spot, between Dover and Calais, in case the notoriously unreliable engines of the time broke down and the pilot had to look for somewhere to land. Landing on land was better that landing at sea.

In March 1917 a pilot flying a Martynside G100 fighter to France had the fright of his life. He was flying along through clear skies, when seemingly from nowhere another British aircraft came screaming down from above in a near-vertical dive. The aircraft was on fire, streaming flames and smoke from its fuselage. The Martynside pilot threw his aircraft into steep diving turn and scanned the skies above for an explanation. Assuming there must be a German fighter around, he twisted and turned for some seconds, but he could see nothing. All that was visible was the smear of smoke left by the doomed aircraft as it plunged down into the sea far below.

Reckoning he had had a narrow escape, the pilot continued on his way and made a report when he landed. A few days later his commanding officer sent for him and questioned him on the incident. Was he sure he had seen an aircraft crash? Was he certain it had been British? Apparently no British aircraft had been reported missing that day.

A few weeks later another pilot had an identical experience. Again there was no plane unaccounted for. Time and again the Ghost Plane of Calais, as the phantom aircraft became known, was seen to plunge into the sea. It was last seen in 1925, long after the war had ended.

The Death of Albert Ball

By May 1917 the top scoring "ace" in the Royal Flying Corps was Captain Albert Ball, a handsome and dashing young man from Nottingham who had gained his pilot's wings in January 1916. He had built up a truly impressive 43 victories in the air, and was a popular pilot with his comrades, though not with his superiors.

On the ground Ball was charming, polite and gregarious company. He often came up with new ideas to pass the time - often involving him playing the violin while others engaged in rumbustious games or pranks - and was always on hand to cheer the lowly mechanics and cooks with jokes and smiles. But in the air, Ball was a loner who displayed a savage determination to kill every German he could find and a complete disregard for orders, discipline or senior officers. In September 1916 he was moved to No.60 Squadron after his commanding officer at No.13 Squadron declared he could no longer stand having Ball under his command.

Albert Ball standing in front of a Caudron G3, a model of reconnaisance aircraft that he never flew in action.

Ball's new commander, Major Barry-Smith, had a long talk with Ball about his attitude to discipline and the needs of the RFC for pilots who would carry out the missions given to them. They came to an arrangement. Ball was given a brand new Nieuport scout aircraft, one of the fastest and most manoeuvrable aircraft in the war. In return for a free hand to fly as he wished, Ball promised to go where he was told and to take two wingmen with him.

In the weeks that followed, Ball chalked up victim after

victim. He developed a deadly technique. He would stalk a victim through the skies, carefully manoeuvring so that he approached the enemy from below and behind without having been seen. He then performed an odd trick that lifted the nose of his aircraft so that he could spray a deluge of bullets at the enemy before they even knew an enemy was about. Quite how he managed this was something of a mystery. He tried to explain to his comrades, but none of them could ever quite get the trick right.

In the winter, Ball was sent home on leave. He took the opportunity to visit Austen and talk to their engineers about the needs of combat pilots. Working closely together, Ball and Austen produced a single seat fighter aircraft which proved to be utterly useless in the air.

Back in France, Ball found that he was now a major celebrity in the RFC. He was posted to No.56 Squadron at Estrée-Blanche where he was given a more modern S.E.5 to fly. Like most pilots, Ball favoured a particular colour scheme - in his case a pure red propeller and boss - so that others could recognise him.

On 7 May Ball was leading his wingmen over Bourlon Wood near Douai. He had orders to keep German aircraft away from a concentration of British troops on the ground. The patrol proved to be eventful for there was a sort fight with German aircraft, which then fled. After resuming the patrol, Ball suddenly waggled his wings. This was the usual way to signal that an enemy aircraft was in sight - none of the aircraft carrying radios at this date. The wingmen looked around, but could see no other aircraft in the skies. Ball then dived suddenly into a cloud bank. The wingmen followed, but when they came out the far side Ball was nowhere to be seen. They stooged about for a while, then flew home.

Ball never returned. He had flown into the cloud bank and vanished.

A week later Ball was officially posted as "Missing". The announcement led to a rash of speculation in the press and among RFC squadrons as to what had happened. Rumours spread like wildfire: A man in a hospital suffering from loss of memory was recognised as Ball: An aircraft had crashed into a river and no body recovered: A red propeller had been found, but no other wreckage.

On 18 May a German aircraft dropped a message canister on to an RFC base. Inside was an announcement from the Imperial German Air Force stating that the body of Albert Ball had been found in a crashed aircraft near Annoeullin on 9 May and had since been buried with full military honours in a war cemetery beside the village church. His grave was marked with a cross on which was inscribed "Fallen in air combat for his fatherland English pilot Captain Albert Ball." Ball, it was claimed, had been shot down by Lothair von Richthofen, younger brother of the more famous Manfred von Richthofen, the Red Baron.

That announcement raised nearly as many questions as it answered. Ball had been some miles from Annoeullin when he vanished, and moreover that village was in the opposite direction from Ball's base. What had he been doing there? The autopsy written by the German doctor who examined Ball's body raised more questions. There were no bullet wounds on the body at all. Death had been caused by massive internal injuries, probably inflicted when the aircraft crashed. There were no burns on the body, so the aircraft had not burned.

When it was discovered that Lothair von Richthofen himself refused to confirm that he had shot down Ball suspicions were raised. Almost certainly the German propaganda ministry had invented the claim after Ball's body was found to boost Lothair's reputation. In fact no German ever claimed to have shot down Ball's S.E.5. So what had happened to Britain's greatest war pilot?

The mystery was never really solved, though there have been many theories. Some said that he must have got disorientated in a cloud and dived into the ground. But such an error was one made by a novice, not an expert pilot.

Some years after the war an English journalist happened to find himself near Annoeullin and decided to go and talk to locals to see if they could shed any light on the matter. Several aircraft had crashed near the village during the war, and the villagers did not know the names of the pilots who died. However, there was one incident that they remembered caused the Germans to get quite agitated.

In the spring of 1917, a British aircraft had got into the habit of zooming past the village church at low level. The aircraft did not come every day, but was a fairly frequent visitor. The villagers thought that perhaps the pilot was checking the time by glancing at the village clock. The local German soldiers also noticed the regular appearance of the British aircraft. An officer ordered them to take a machine gun up to the church tower and take a shot at the aircraft next time it turned up.

A few days later, the villagers could not agree on the exact date, the aircraft came back. The machine gun opened fire, riddled the aircraft with bullets and sent it plunging out of control into a nearby field. A woman had dashed to the crash and pulled the pilot from the wreckage. He was still alive and had no obvious injuries, but he was coughing up blood and died in her arms a few minutes later.

The German troops were jubilant and took possession of both the crash and the body. However, when air force officers turned up the mood turned dark. This was why the villagers remembered the incident. The air force officers at first acted routinely, but when one of them looked at the dead pilot's wallet he turned suddenly angry. There followed a blazing row between the airmen and the local soldiers. Eventually the air force men drove off with the dead pilot's body. No more was ever said of the incident.

Was Albert Ball the victim of the machine gun in the church tower. We will probably never know, but what the villagers recalled of the incident does seem to fit the few facts that are known.

The Piper of Polygon Wood

ANOTHER STORY THAT WAS PASSED FROM MOUTH TO MOUTH along the British lines was that of the Piper of Polygon Wood. Unlike the Angel of Mons or the Gurkha with the Silver Kukri nearly every recorded version of this tale places it firmly in both place and time: October 1917 at Polygon Wood, a large stretch of woodland near Zonnebeke to the east of Ypres.

The joint British-Australian attack was intended to capture the devastated woodland and secure the high ground beyond. If the Broodseinde Ridge could be captured, British artillery would be able to dominate the German supply lines. The Germans felt that the position was safe. Not only had shellfire brought down nearly all the trees, creating a nightmare tangle of fallen logs and snagging branches, but the drainage channels had been smashed and the ground was excessively muddy. However the few days before the attack went in were unseasonably hot and dry, giving the British troops firm land to advance over.

As usual the attack was timed for dawn and preceded by an artillery barrage. By this date the tactics of advance had been refined. The artillery barrage was not only properly targetted at German strongpoints, but moved slowly at walking pace, so that the advancing infantry could walk behind it and so gain shelter

British soldiers advancing into battle near Polygon Wood in 1917 when aircraft of the RFC patrol overhead.

from the German defences. Even so, attacking over No Man's Land was a horrifically dangerous thing to do.

On the morning of the attack the men of the 42nd Royal Highland Regiment - better known by their nickname of the Black Watch - were getting ready to attack. Men were nervously checking their rifles, sharpening their bayonets and waiting for the officer's whistle that would send them scrambling up the parapet for the desperate charge across the desolate waste of No Man's Land to fight the Germans. The artillery bombardment boomed from behind them, then crashed down on the German lines ahead.

Suddenly a different sound was to be heard. It was a toneless moan at first, a dreary wail, but as it gathered in strength it gained clarity and could soon be heard for what it was - the bagpipes.

Scottish regiments at this date were still wearing kilts, and for the charge against the Germans they preferred the traditional glengarry cap to the cumbersome steel helmet, but bagpipes had long since been moved off the battlefield. There were plenty of pipers and bagpipes in France, but they played only when the regiments were in rear areas resting from their turns of duty in the front lines. When the Scots went into the trenches they left their pipes behind them.

And yet hundreds of men of the Black Watch could now clearly hear a piper playing the regimental march of "Highland Laddie".

A sentry grabbed a periscope to peer up over the parapet. After scanning the area for some time, he beckoned over an officer and passed him the periscope. Then he turned to his fellows.

"It's a piper," he said. "A pipe major in full tartan rig. He's marching up and down out there." He gestured toward No Man's Line. "Marching up and down playing his pipes like he was on parade."

"Why don't the Germans shoot him?" someone asked.

"I don't think they can see him," replied the sentry.

All eyes turned to the officer, but at that moment whistles sounded along the trench. The officer glanced down at his watch, hurriedly blew his own whistle and led the scramble up and over the top. The Black Watch stormed forward, screaming and yelling as they raced to get over the deadly open spaces of No Man's Land and get to grips with the enemy.

The pipe major, his dress tartan kilt swinging as he walked moved on steadly ahead of them. Some men saw him leap over the first German trench, but then the Black Watch were in among the Germans and fighting hand to hand. They lost sight of the pipe major, though the skirling wail of the pipes continued to sound for some time. Gradually the sound faded, as if the pipe major were marching away out of earshot. Then the sound was gone altogether.

After the action, the men discussed what they had seen. Everyone agreed that they had seen a pipe major in the regimental tartan playing the regimental march. No such man was to be found. A search was made up and down the line, but neither a living nor a dead piper was to be found.

Then one old soldier spoke up. He had not wanted to say anything until then, he said, for he feared the men would laugh at him. He said he had recognised the piper as Piper John MacDonald. Clear as day, the old soldier said, it was Piper MacDonald who had been with the regiment for thirty years until he died of some disease in a hospital the previous summer. The men shifted uneasily.

Whether he was ghost or human, the Piper of Polygon Wood was never found alive or dead. And other than the man who thought the piper had been John MacDonald, nobody claimed to have recognised him. But the Black Watch were led into battle that grim October morning by a figure who became known up and down the lines as The Phantom Pipler of Polygon Wood.

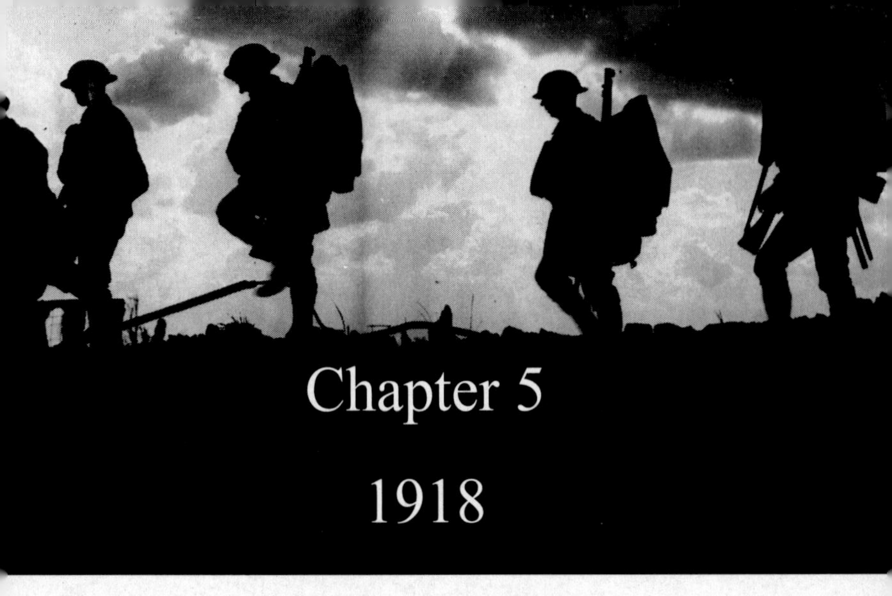

Chapter 5

1918

The Cursed U-boat

IN JULY 1918 THE GERMAN SUBMARINE U-boat 65 went missing. She had been sent on a mission to patrol the seas of southwest England and southern Ireland. These were rich hunting grounds for the U-boats for merchant men had to use these waters to get into and out of southern British ports. That the U-boat did not return was a disappointment to the Germans, but was no great mystery. When U-boats were sunk by the British they rarely had time to get a message off by radio to say that they were under attack. Indeed, radio silence was important, so the Imperial Germany Navy did not expect to hear directly that a U-boat had been lost. They might get a report from newspapers in neutral countries such as Norway or the Netherlands, or there again they might not.

However, U-boat 65 was no ordinary U-boat. She was widely rumoured to be cursed and haunted. When news spread through the navy that she had been lost, nobody was very surprised.

U-boat 65 was one of the very latest and most modern submarines in the German navy. She belonged to the UBIII class of attack submarines that were designed to operate in the coastal waters off western Britain. Like her fellow Type UBIII craft she displaced 555 tonnes was 56 metres long and had a top speed of 14 knots on the surface or 8 knots submerged. She had four torpedo tubes, carrying ten torpedoes in all, and had a 88mm gun on her deck. Taken together she was fast, modern and deadly. She should have been an asset to the Imperial German Navy, but in fact she was a liability.

U-boat 65 was commissioned on 18 August 1917, but she already had a sinister reputation. On the day her keel was laid down a chain securing a heavy girder to a crane came undone. The girder crashed down, killing a workman who was in the construction bay. An inspection of the chain followed, but there seemed to be nothing wrong with it.

Some weeks later as the submarine neared completion fumes were seen coming out of the engine room. For some reason the dry cell batteries had malfunctioned and begun producing poisonous gas. The three engineeers in the engine room were all killed. The batteries were tested, but nothing could be found wrong with them.

The shipbuilders blamed the short timescale that the navy had given them for completion of the new U-boats that were needed so desperately for the war against Britain. The navy said the shipbuilders were making excuses for sloppy work and told them to get on with it.

Whether Captain Martin Schelle knew of the four deaths that had already taken place on his new command is not known, but certainly he did not pass the information on to his crew.

Soon after she was commissioned, Schelle took the U-boat 65 out for her sea trials. When a strong wind blew up, Schelle decided to take advantage of it to test the submarines ability to stay stable in rough seas. The ship did well, so Schelle sent a man to check the hatches and other external fixtures. For no apparent the reason the man slipped and fell overboard. His comrades threw a float, but there was no sign of him. He had sunk like a stone.

Things got even worse on the first cruise out into the North Sea. During a routine diving exercise one of the ballast tanks cracked, letting in a flood of seawater. The submarine sank to the bottom of the sea. For more than 12 hours the submarine remained stubbornly stuck. With oxygen rapidly running out Schelle and his engineer finally found a way to give the craft enough bouyancy to return to the surface. It was only by the narrowest of margins that the craft got to base safely.

As the U-boat 65 prepared for its first operational cruise to attack shipping in the English Channel, there was a powerful blast in the forward part of the submarine. One of the torpedo warheads had detonated. The second officer, Lieutenant Richter

A pair of Type UBIII U-boats deliberately beached by their crews at the end of the war.

was killed. The crew attended the funeral, then went on leave while the damage was repaired.

When the submarine was being prepared to go to sea some weeks later, Captain Schelle found himself approached by a white-faced crew member who said he had just seen the ghost of Second Officer Richter walking up the gang plank. Reasoning the man may be hung over from shore leave and had mistaken some other officer for the dead man, the Captain advised the man to have a lie down and then get back to work.

Shortly afterwards another crew member came to the captain and reported that he had seen the ghost standing on the bows of the U-boat. Once the U-boat was at sea, a third crew member claimed to have seen the ghost inspecting the instrument panel in the engineering section.

Despite such alarms, the first cruise proved to be a success, so did those that followed. In all U-boat 65 carried out six cruises, sinking a confirmed six merchant ships and one war sloop, HMS Arbutus. She also hit six other merchant ships, but without sinking them.

Successful as U-boat 65 seemed to be, she could not shake off the rumours of a curse, and the hauntings continued. Captain Schelle stuck with his ship, though crew members put in for transfers rather more frequently than on other ships. And some crew members risked court martial rather than put to sea.

One of those who did go to sea suffered a nervous breakdown saying that the ghost had walked past his hammock every night, moving toward the torpedo room where Richter had died.

It is said that even Captain Schelle saw the ghost on one occasion. He and a seaman were in the conning tower one day as the submarine ploughed its way through stormy seas. Waves broke over the low decks of the craft, washing over the deck gun and surging to break against the tower. The seaman then saw what he took to be a member of the crew standing near the bows. Wondering why on earth a man would be standing in such a dangerous place he drew the captain's attention to the figure.

Captain Schelle gazed forward to where the man stood and shouted at him. Then the man turned to face the conning tower. It was Lieutenant Richter - or rather his ghost. The crewman gasped and turned to the captain. Schelle stared silently at the ghost and gripped the rail of the conning tower tighter and tighter until his knuckled turned white - but he said not a word.

When U-boat 65 docked at the end of that that cruise, Captain Schelle sent the entire crew ashore for the day. He did not tell them the reason for the move, but word was soon being passed around the harbour. While the crew were gone a priest had come to see Captain Schelle and then the two men had gone on board the submarine. An hour or so later the priest left. Schelle never explained what had happened, but everyone assumed that he had asked to priest to exorcise the submarine.

It was on the very next voyage, the seventh, that U-boat 65 was lost.

For many years it was thought that the submarine had been lost off the south coast of Ireland. On 10 July the US Submarine L-2 was near Fastnet Rock when the lookout spotted a periscope. There was then a sudden underwater explosion, after which the hydrophone operator heard the sound of small propellers. This seemed to indicate that a submarine had sunk. As U-boat 65 was the only craft lost that was operating in the waters, it was assumed that this was what had happened.

In 2004, however, a routine survey off the north coast of Cornwall found a wrecked U-boat off the mouth of the Camel Estuary, not far from the fishing port of Padstow. Channel 4 Television sponsored an investigation as part of a series they were making on underwater archaeology and the wreck was identified as that of U-boat 65.

Records showed that a Portuguese merchant ship had been

torpedoed just up the coast on 14 July 1918. Presumably U-boat 65 had carried out that attack and then sunk soon afterwards. An investigation of the wreck revealed no obvious damage, nor did records show any Royal Navy ship launching any sort of an attack on a suspected U-boat in the area at that time.

Several of the rear hatches were open, indicating that the crew had tried to escape as the U-boat was sinking. Clearly nobody managed to survive. The cause of the sinking of U-boat 65 remains a total mystery. All 37 men on board had died.

Whether the submarine actually was cursed or haunted is an open question. Certainly she came to a strange and unexplained end.

The Female Flyer

In February 1918 a German pilot shot down alive behind British lines was taken in for the usual questioning. The British officers plied him with the usual questions about German aircraft, dispositions and strength. The German replied with the usual stoic refusal to say anything other than confirm his name, rank and number.

The surprise came when the interview ended and the German was about to be led away. He stopped and requested permission to ask a question. The British officers glanced at each other, then nodded their assent.

"Would it be possible for you to introduce me to the young lady who shot me down?" asked the German.

"Young lady?" gasped the British officers.

The German confirmed that he did mean a woman, and then went on to tell the astonished British officers that every German pilot in that section of the line knew that one British squadron counted a young woman among its pilots. Many German airmen had seen her, some of them at very close quarters. She was young, had long blonde hair and, so far as could be seen past the flying goggles and sheepskin jacket, was uncommonly pretty.

The interrogation began all over again, except this time the British wanted to know all about the lady flyer. Now it was the German's turn to be surprised. Surely the British intelligence officers knew all about the girl. Some Germans, he said, thought she was the sister of Albert Ball, a girl named Lois. She had learned to fly had she not? The Female Flyer must be her, come out to France to seek revenge for her brother's death. Whoever she was, she flew a Sopwith Triplane and the Germans credited her with having shot down at least a dozen aircraft.

News of this extraordinary interview spread like wildfire among the RFC squadrons. Everyone was asking everyone else if the pretty female pilot was in their squadron, while everyone denied that she was in their unit.

Fairly soon she began to be seen by British pilots as well as by Germans. She was seen flying an S.E.5 and a Camel, she was seen shooting down a German reconnaissance aircraft. She blasted to pieces a German fighter as it pounced on a British bomber. She was here, she was there, she was everywhere and yet she was nowhere for no squadron admitted to having a woman on its strength. She was still being seen by both British and German airmen as the war came to an end in November 1918.

The solution to this particular mystery has never really been found. However, the fact that British airmen started to report the Female Flyer only after the captured German pilot asked about her might suggest one explanation. Aircraft, even those in service in World War I, fly at high speeds. Aircraft might pass each other at a combined speed of some 300 miles per hour. At those sorts of speeds a pilot would get only the most fleeting of glimpses of the other aircraft and its pilot. Perhaps a pilot who knew of the story of the Female Flyer caught a dash of colour out of the corner of his eye and thought it was long blonde hair, when in fact it was a fluttering scarf.

This is only guesswork, but so far as is known there were no women flying with the RFC in 1918 - and yet dozens of pilots were convinced that they saw her. Presumably they were seeing something. Perhaps even a young woman pilot.

Who killed the Red Baron

ON 21 APRIL 1918 THE MOST FAMOUS PILOT of the First World War was shot down and killed. At the time of his death the Red Baron, as he was known, had claimed 80 enemy aircraft. Although his aircraft came down intact and there was no doubt as to his identity, there has always been dispute over just who it was who shot down the great Baron Manfred von Richthofen.

Born in 1892, Richthofen began the war in a cavalry regiment on the Eastern Front, but in 1915 he transferred to the Imperial Air Service. At first he flew as an observer in two-seater aircraft on reconnaissance missions, performing pretty much the same role for which he had been trained in the cavalry though this time from the air. In September 1915 he chanced to meet Oswald Boelcke, then the greatest fighter ace in the world and one of the leading theoreticians of air combat. Inspired, Richthofen applied for pilot training and pulled strings to get himself posted to Boelcke's squadron. On his first flight with Boelcke he crashed his aircraft due to an incompetent landing.

Getting over his bad start, Richthofen shot down his first victim on 26 April 1916 - a French Neiuport Scout. From

A modern replica of the Fokker DrI with which the Red Baron is forever linked in the popular imagination.
Photo by Matthias Kabel

Boelcke, Richthofen learned a set of simple insturctions that he passed on to colleagues and, when he got to command his own squadron, he had posted up in the mess. Richthofen was never an outstanding pilot, but he was a superb shot and a master of tactics. He never risked himself or other pilots in rash attacks or risky missions. Instead he dedicated himself to the slow but certain destruction of enemy aircraft, carefully setting up the circumstances in which victory would be almost certain, and evading dangerous situations.

For most of his career, Richthofen flew various models of the Albatros fighter. However, he is best known for flying the Fokker Dr.I triplane. He claimed 19 of his 80 victims flying the triplane. Although the Fokker was highly manoeuvrable, it was rather slow and most German pilots preferred the Albatros.

In the spring of 1917 Richthofen took command of Jasta 11. Within days all his pilots paid tribute to their new leader by painting some prominent part of their aircraft the same shade of brilliant red favoured by their leader. In June he was put in command of a four squadron unit that was officially known as a "Jagdgeschwader", but was informally called a "Flying Circus" by both sides. The Circus was a highly mobile unit able to pack its maintenance gear, spare parts and support equipment into trucks at a moment's notice to move to whatever section of the line needed additional aerial firepower.

On 6 July 1917 Richthofen sustained a severe head injury when a bullet grazed his skull causing fractures and bone splinters. He was out of service until 23 October, and on his return suffered from headaches at altitude. His superior officers urged him to stand down from combat flying and take a senior position that would involve desk duties, but he refused.

On 21 April 1918, Richthofen was leading a routine patrol when his squadron attacked a formation of Sopwith Camels from the British No.209 Squadron. Richthofen singled out an aircraft flown by Canadian Lieutenant Wilfred May and got on to its tail. May put his nose down to dive for speed and headed toward the front lines to get over British-held territory.

At this date the Germans were advancing quickly as part of their great Spring Offensive of 1918, so none of the pilots would have been entirely certain where the front lines on the ground actually were.

Richthofen followed May down to very low level - something that he had frequently warned his fellow pilots against doing as it restricted their freedom of movement if they got into trouble. And Richthofen was very soon in trouble. Diving down on him from behind and to the left came another No.209 Squadron Sopwith Camel, flown by Captain Arthur Brown. Brown fired a long burst, hitting the German aircraft several times. He saw

Richthofen jink violently to avoid the attack, then climbed back upward to regain height.

As Brown manoeuvred ready to attack again he saw Richthofen continue to follow May for about a minute. Then Richthofen's aircraft turned aside and landed violently in a field near Vaux-sur-Somme. A dozen Australian soldiers from a nearby artillery unit ran to the downed aircraft. Among the first men to arrive was a medical Sergeant Ted Smout. He saw that Richthofen had a wound in his chest that was bleeding freely. Richthofen grimaced, said a single word "kaput" and then passed out. Within seconds he was dead.

A subsequent post mortem found that he had been killed by a single 0.303 bullet that entered his body under his right arm and exited from his left chest. It had smashed through his lungs and severed important blood vessels close to his heart. Death would have followed within a minute or so.

The British at once credited Brown with having shot down the Red Baron, and announced the news to the world. The death came as a morale blow to the German people.

The Red Baron's body was given a full military funeral by the men of the neareast squadrons to where his aircraft had come down, No.3 Squadron of the Australian Flying Corps. The funeral was attended by large numbers of Allied pilots and numerous squadron sent wreaths in tribute. The funeral was filmed and a copy of the film sent to Germany by way of a neutral country.

After the war Richthofen's younger brother Bolko had the body moved to Berlin where it recieved a full State Funeral and was interred in the famous Invalidenfriedhof Cemetery alongside kings, princes and other heroes.

Meanwhile, Brown had proved to be remarkably modest about his feat of having shot down the famous Red Baron. When cornered by an insistent newspaper reporter and asked to describe the combat he replied only "There is no point in me commenting, as the evidence is already out there".

At the same time rumours abounded that Brown had not fired the fatal shot at all. In his combat report, Brown said he had attacked Richthofen from above and from the left, yet the fatal bullet had come from the right. Of course, pilots do move about in the cockpit, but not that much. The officers of the Australian 24th Machine Gun Company were soon claiming that one of their men had shot down the Red Baron. Sergeant Cedric Popkin had fired at the Red Baron twice that day. He fired first as the aircraft was coming directly at him, then a second time as it circled back while chasing May. On the second occasion Popkin had been firing from Richthofen's right, the direction from which the fatal shot had come.

Another claim came from Gunner Snowy Evans of the Australian 14th Field Artillery Brigade. He too had fired at Richthofen from the right side as he chased after May. However, Evans had fired early in the chase and the nature of the wounds meant that it was unlikely that Richthofen would have been able to continue his chase of May after being wounded.

Neither of the Australian claims came out in public as the authorities were keen to credit the destruction of the Red Baron to a pilot, and so Brown got the credit. Nevertheless, the rumours continued to circulate.

Puzzles also persisted over Richthofen's behaviour on the fatal day. He had repeatedly told his pilots never to go down low over enemy ground troops. He had also cautioned constantly that it was better to allow an enemy aircraft to escape rather than put yourself at risk. And yet Richthofen had done both these things, and it had ended in his death. It has been suggested that his head wound of 1917 had affected his judgment and behaviour - though nothing unusual had been noticed before his fatal flight.

In 1998 an exhaustive investigation into the question was conducted by military historian Geoffrey Miller. He concluded that Popkin had fired the fatal shot. So far nobody has disputed those findings.

The Phantom Observer

In February 1918 a pilot in an RFC squadron in France asked for a transfer to another squadron. The pilot was a good, steady man and his commanding officer was reluctant to lose him. He said he would discuss the matter, but in the meantime asked the pilot to continue to fly artillery spotting missions in his R.E.8 two seater aircraft.

The C.O. was aware that the pilot had recently lost his long term Observer in strange circumstances. The two had been on a routine mission over the lines spotting for British artillery. Everything had seemed to go well. The pilot stooged about, keeping a wary eye open for German aircraft, while the observer located the fall of shot and radioed the results back to the artillery battery.

When the mission ended the R.E.8 had flown back to base without incident and taxied up to the hangars. It was only when the pilot climbed out of the cockpit that he realised that the observer was stone dead. The body had no injuries and there was no explanation for the sudden death.

Perhaps, the C.O. thought, the incident was preying on the mind of the pilot. He gave the man leave and hoped that on his return he would feel better. If anything the man was worse. He slept badly and would jump if someone crept up behind him. Eventually the pilot confided to a friend that the ghost of his observer was haunting him. The observer had had a distinctive laugh, and the pilot heard that laugh whenever he got in to the aircraft.

A routine part of a pilot's life in 1918 was to test fly his aircraft to ensure that the wires and struts were all secure and operating properly. A week after his return from leave the pilot climbed in to his aircraft for one such test flight. As he did so he stopped to stare at the empty observer's seat, then nodded and started the engine. The aircraft took off smoothly enough, but never returned to base. Its burnt out wreckage was found later that day a few miles away.

The Surrey Soccer Player

On 8 August 1918 the British launched an offensive that would last 100 days and finally bring victory to the Allies. For weeks the British had been battered by repeated German offensives, and been pushed back for miles. But now the Germans had run out of supplies and reinforcements. It was the British turn to attack.

The place chosen for the opening offensive was Amiens. The ground was firm and open, which made it ideal for a startling new tactic dreamed up by General Henry Rawlinson of the 4th Army. Instead of the usual days-long bombardment of enemy positions by artillery, the infantry would go over the top entirely unannounced - but they would advance alongside the lumbering armoured vehicles known as tanks. These tanks had been used before, but Rawlinson sent forward nearly 600 of them in a swarm that would be impervious to German machine guns and light artillery, opening up the way for the infantry to follow. Secrecy was vital. Rawlinson called on the Royal Flying Corps to drive the German aircraft from the skies over Amiens so that no prowling German pilot would see the huge numbers of men and tanks being massed behind the lines.

On the morning of 8 August the tanks lumbered forward, firing their guns at anything that moved and rolling flat the German barbed wire entanglements.

In one section of the lines the East Surrey Regiment scrambled over the parapet and charged forward into No Man's Land. Standing amid the flattened barbed wire waiting for them was a familiar figure: Terry Weldon. Weldon had been a familiar figure in the regiment, having played football for Croydon and for England before the war. He was not with the regiment, being sick behind the lines. But now here he was, and he had a football tucked under his arm. He waved the men forward, then turned toward the German lines, booting the football ahead of him.

The East Surreys gained their objective easily, as did all the attacking regiments that day. German morale was at rock bottom, and the massed tanks had been the last straw. Thousands of German soldiers surrendered in what the German commander Erich Ludendorff famously called "The Black Day of the German Army". The British ended the day seven miles behind what had been the German front line. Ludendorff told the politicians back in Berlin that it was time to seek an armistice.

Resting after the action, the East Surreys looked around for Weldon. He was nowhere to be seen. Next day news came that he had died in hospital early the previous morning - just as so many men saw him lead the attack.

The Kaiser's Last Soldier

The First World War is generally reckoned to have ended with the Armistice of 11 November 1918. However the last German military unit to remain in the field did not surrender until 5 January 1919, and mystery has surrounded the event ever since. The controversy began almost as soon as Hermann Detzner marched out of the New Guinea jungle resplendent in his full dress uniform and followed by a small column of a couple of dozen German troops.

Detzner trained as a surveyor and engineer. He undertook a number of expeditions for the German government to map remote areas of Africa, accepting a commission as a lieutenant in the German army as a way to get paid and gain the rank and prestige needed to gain co-operation from colonial officials.

In January 1914 Detzner was sent to New Guinea to map out the borders between the lands claimed by Germany - then called Kaiser-Wilhelmsland - and the lands claimed by the British and Dutch. After some preliminary work laying his plans, Detzner set off up the Ono River with 25 men, 45 carriers, 2 servants and an interpreter. He stayed in touch with the German colonial authorities by means of runners who went back and forth with messages and supplies.

On 11 November one runner came back carrying a note written by Fredrick Chisholm of the Australian army. This informed Detzner that the war had begun, that the German authorities and troops in Kaiser-Wilhelmsland had surrendered after a short battle and instructed Detzner to likewise surrender. After considering his options, Detzner decided not to surrender. His duty, he believed, was to stay free, cause the Allies as much trouble as he could and so tie down Allied soldiers who would otherwise have been free to be used elsewhere.

For the next few months, Detzner led his men on an arduous march through the mountainous jungles of the interior, passing through the Langimar Valley, on to the Huon Peninsula, over the Saruwaged Mountains and elsewhere. His primary objective during these months was to reach the more isolated German outposts before the Allies and so add to his command the handful of German soldiers and policemen that were to be found. In March 1915 he left some of his men who were sick with malaria to be captured and cared for by the Australians, then he headed back into the interior.

Over the months and years that followed, the Australians heard stories from local tribesmen of Detzner's travels and activities. They sent out frequent patrols to follow up on these reports, but wherever they went the German remained on step ahead of them. They arrived only after he had gone, and very often failed to find any trace of him and his men at all. Nevertheless, Detzner was clearly fulfilling his mission of keeping Allied troops on New Guinea chasing him when they would have been more useful elsewhere.

In 1917 an Australian civilian saw Detzner and some men paddling canoes along the north coast of New Guinea, apparently trying to reach the neutral Dutch colony to the west. By the time troops could arrive the canoe had vanished and Detzner was nowhere to be seen.

When word arrived in New Guinea in November 1918 that the war was over, the Australians told the local tribesmen that they should tell Detzner that the war was over and that he could come out of the interior. Thus it was the Detzner marched out of the jungles, having changed into his carefully preserved full dress uniform, and surrendered at Finschhafen.

After a short stay in Australia, Detzner was allowed to go back to Germany where he received a hero's welcome. Not only that but he found he had been promoted to the rank of Major and loaded with honours. Honours, however, do not pay the bills so Detzner wrote a book entitled "Four Years among the Cannibals, from 1914 to the Armistice, under the German Flag, in the Unexplored Interior of New Guinea". It was an immediate sensation and sold in large numbers, so he followed it up with memoirs about his earlier travels in Africa. The books were translated into several languages and Detzner went on speaking tours around the world. At home his popularity was boosted by patriotic asides asserting that the locals in New Guinea much preferred German paternalistic rule to the alleged exploitation of their new Australian rulers. The scientific community, meanwhile, was agog as his books and lectures revealed new species of bird and mammal and unknown facts about New Guinea geology and geography.

The only slight fly in the ointment was that Detzner was very vague about exactly where he and his men and gone and what they had done. He talked about rivers, hills and mountains but did not reveal when he had been where. Detzner claimed this was to protect the local tribesmen who had helped him from revenge from the brutal Australians.

The Australians were, understandably, annoyed by this. They protested loudly, claiming that it had been Detzner, not they, who had persecuted the locals who had been only too happy to see the backs of the Germans. Several Australian soldiers came forward to deny that Hetzner had caused them any real problems at all. They said that they had known all the time roughly where he was, mostly on the Huon Peninsula, and that they had left him alone as he was causing no trouble.

The controversy rumbled on, but the truth remained elusive.

Then, in 1929 the German missionary Christian Keyser returned home to Germany on his retirement. He read Detzner's book and exploded with rage. Keyser claimed that a large proportion of Hetzner's discoveries had actually been made by himself and some missionary colleagues. It was they, Keyser said, who had discovered new species, collected rock samples and mapped the land. Neither man had documentary evidence of their claims, so it was difficult for others to know who to believe. By 1932, however, other missionaries were writing to

German newspapers and institutions to support Keyser. Gradually the truth came out.

Throughout his years "in the jungle" Detzner had in fact been staying with a succession of plantation owners, missionaries and traders - mostly on the Huon Peninsula. His tales of extensive wanderings in the interior of New Guinea were simple fabrications. Detzner explained that he had at first made up the tale of his journeys to protect those who had helped him from Australian revenge. Others, he said, had spread the story long before he got home to Germany. His book, he said, had been written to further protect those who had helped him and he pointed out that he had been deliberately vague about what he had done to avoid telling any actual lies.

The immediate result was to utterly discredit Detzner and his book. He retired from private life and took up a position in the publishing industry. But the controversy did not end there. A review of the book "Four Years among the Cannibals, from 1914 to the Armistice, under the German Flag, in the Unexplored Interior of New Guinea" in the 1990s showed that much of what Detzner had written was substantially true.

The Blame Game

Perhaps the final mystery of the First World War is, ultimately, one of the easiest to solve and yet the most tragic of them all.

When the war was over the Allies, and in particular the French, were vociferous in blaming the Germans for the outbreak of the war. The fighting stopped with the armistice of 11 November 1918, but Germany was then left in limbo for some months over what was going to happen next. It was usual for the two sides at the end of a war to enter into negotiations over what the peace terms were going to be. These terms might include the defeated state handing over territory or money to the victor. There would normally be a good deal of wrangling over the actual conditions.

This is undoubtedly what the Germans expected to happen in 1918. Instead they were left hanging about while the Allies decided what they wanted. The armistice had included an agreement that German troops would leave all occupied territory and that Allied troops would be based in key places throughout Germany. It was not until 18 April 1919 that the German government was invited to send a delegation to Versailles to finalise the peace arrangements.

The Germans sent Count Ulrich von Brodkdorff-Rantzau along with 180 staff, including economic, geographic and industrial experts who expected to be called upon to discuss a host of technical details. But when Brodkdorff-Rantzau arrived he was told bluntly that there would be no talks. He was given the text of the Versailles Treaty, agreed by the Allies, and told he had 15 days to sign it or the war would begin again.

Brodkdorff-Rantzau took the treaty back to Berlin, then resigned his position. The head of the German government, Philip Scheidermann also resigned. It was not until 22 June that a new government willing to sign the peace treaty could be formed.

The prime sticking point was what became known as the "War Guilt Clause". It was clause 231 and read:

"The Allied and Associated Governments affirm and Germany accepts the responsibility of Germany and her allies for causing all the loss and damage to which the Allied and Associated Governments and their nationals have been subjected as a consequence of the war imposed upon them by the aggression of Germany and her allies."

When Brodkdorff-Rantzau first read this phrase he was aghast. He told French Prime Minister George Clemenceau "We know the full brunt of hate that confronts us here. You demand from us to confess we were the only guilty party of war; such a confession in my mouth would be a lie."

The Germans themselves felt very strongly that they had not caused the war. The Kaiser had certainly been at pains to try to persuade the Austro-Hungarians to be moderate in their response to the assassination of Archduke Franz Ferdinand. Once the Austrians had issued their ultimatum, the Kaiser urged them to accept the Serb response. If anyone was to blame for the outbreak of the war, the Germans thought, it was either the Serbs or the Austrians. Clause 231 was widely seen in Germany as a national humiliation and an attempt to make Germany sign away its honour.

It was primarily the French who drove the insistence on Clause 231. Neither the British nor American negotiators seem to have been particularly keen on it, and the smaller Allies such as Romania were not consulted. So the mystery arising out of the Versailles Treaty is this. Why did the Allies so obviously and so insistently blame Germany for the outbreak of the war, when all the evidence would indicate that it was not Germany which had done so.

The reason why the French were so determined to blame Germany for the war was simple: Money.

Large areas of northern France had been devastated by the fighting and by the German occupation. This included the most industrially advanced parts of France, economically important areas the French could not afford to lose. The French referred to the area of land devastated by the war as "Zone Rouge". They claimed that 460 square miles of France had been utterly destroyed and listed the villages and towns that had been razed. The claimes may have been exaggerated, but the devastation had been widespread. Due to the presence of huge quantities of unexploded artillery shells large areas of land were closed, and even in the 21st century some small areas remain sealed off.

If Germany was blamed for the war, then Germany could be made to pay for the damage done to France. There was no point blaming the Austro-Hungarian Empire, arguably the true culprits, as that Empire had ceased to exist. It had broken up into several smaller states such as Czechoslovakia, Hungary, Yugoslavia and Austria - none of which could be blamed as they had not existed. Similarly, the Ottoman Empire and collapsed and ceased to exist. Bulgaria was too small and poor to pay anything much. That left Germany.

Not only did France want German cash. They had another motive. if Germany could be impoverished it was unlikely that it would be in a position to be able to invade France again. So not only was Germany forbidden to have a large army or modern weapons of war, it was also economically undermined. That was possible only if Germany could be blamed.

In the event the Versailles Treaty proved to be both harsh and lenient. It was harsh in that it blamed Germany for the war and extracted massive amounts of money and payment in kind. It was lenient in that it left Germany largely intact as a country and as an industrial powerhouse. It therefore combined giving great insult to the German people with leaving them with the means to seek redress.

It was a mistake that would have terrible repercussions in 1939.